Canadian
LEGAL FORMS LTD.

MW01222252

Business
Forms

Canada

C.G.T. Canadian Legal Forms Ltd
Burnaby, B.C. / service@CanadaForms.com

Business Forms
© Copyright 2001 C.G.T. Canadian Legal Forms LTD
P.O. Box 82664
Burnaby, B.C. V5C 5W4
service@CanadaForms.com

1 2 3 4 5 6 7 8 9 10

This publication is designed to provide accurate and authoritative information in regard to subject matter covered. It is sold with the understanding that neither the publisher nor author is engaged in rendering legal, accounting, or other professional services. If legal advice or other expert assistance is required, the services of a competent professional should be sought.

Business Forms

Important Notice

This product is intended for informational use only and is not a substitute for legal advice. Provincial laws vary and change, and the information or forms do not necessarily conform to the laws or requirements of your province. While you always have the right to prepare your own documents and to act as your own lawyer, do consult a lawyer on all important legal matters. This product was not necessarily prepared by a person licensed to practice law in your province.

TABLE OF CONTENTS

Alphabetical Listing of Forms

-A-

-B-

-C-

-D-

-E-

-F-

-G

-H-

-I-

-P-

-Q-

-R-

-S-

-T-

Categorical Listing of Forms

1. Planning and Organization

2. Executive and Administrative

3. Accounting and Finance

4. Personnel

5. Projects

6. Purchasing and Shipping

7. *Sales and Marketing*

8. *Columnar Templates*

9. Blank Grids

Introduction

Business Forms for Managing Your Business

Technology may run the modern office, but you continue to do the work—and good business records are essential. With the right business forms, you can avoid costly mistakes, maintain client goodwill, handle major business decisions, and achieve your business goals with a minimum of time and money. Select from the enclosed forms, use all the forms or just those you need—terrific as templates or worksheets—you'll be more organized, and experience greater business security with the right forms for your business, right now.

Planning and Organization

Take control of your time. You can easily customize your daily, weekly, monthly, or yearly planning—select from a choice of ready-to-complete perpetual checklists, calendars, charge sheets, appointment records, or blank columnar templates. With your chosen planner, you will never be late for an appointment again. Planners help you keep track of appointments, contacts, and pending to-do items. C.G.T. Canadian Legal Forms planners provide a fast, easy and effective complete time management system. Each to-do task may be priority coded. You can assign tasks to any project and/or to a person responsible for a task. These powerful, easy-to-use planners organize your most important tasks and appointments.

Projects

Project records provide a great way to summarize key information, and to manage people and resources. Use the *Project Plan* or *Project Schedule* to simplify your project management tasks—from employee scheduling, equipment, room or facilities scheduling, to managing a project team. Whether you need to schedule resources by the day, the hour or the year, planners reduce the time and effort spent scheduling and help improve your resource utilization. Delegate and prioritize job tasks and stay on track, on time, and on budget. C.G.T. Canadian Legal Forms planners enable you to:

- quickly estimate potential resource requirements and schedules
- immediately see your project(s) cost
- view a variety of pre-built reports to aid your own decision-making

Executive and Administrative

Customize your business' essential operations forms for highest efficiency from a selection of ready-to-use C.G.T. Canadian Legal Forms executive and administrative forms. Streamline office procedures with these carefully researched and tested forms. Select from a variety of forms that help you manage all facets of office control from maintaining an essential contact directory to ordering parts and inventory control. Whether your company has one or two major clients or hundreds, the basic needs remain unchanged. Your company must maintain payroll, order supplies, and send correspondence. Keep track using the *Inventory Control* and *Out of Stock Notice*. Maintain essential numbers with the *Telephone / Fax Log*. Over 40 indispensable forms make it easier for you to run your business efficiently.

Accounting and Finance

The most affordable and efficient way to manage daily office expenses and revenue, *Business Forms* includes an essential selection of forms. Record vendor payments, credit history, cash flow budgets, and other required office expense records. Flexible and easy to use, small business accounting need not cost a fortune. Data may be readily changed at any time and, whether you sell goods or services, it is easy to record vendor information. You can apply for credit, notify customers of past due bills, keep track of your budget, reconcile daily cash, and run a financial trend analysis.

Purchasing and Shipping

Track your products and manage your purchase order requests using the purchasing and shipping forms. The forms provide spacing to maintain running and cumulative totals. Also provide an easy client quote with shipping costs, tax, and net discount percentages.

Sales and Marketing

Track leads, contacts, and results involved in your sales and marketing efforts with the sales, telemarketing, and direct mail forms provided with *Business Forms*. The simple, ready-to-use forms, will help you attain and retain customers, track your marketing and advertising efforts, and view the results. Quickly see how effective your direct mail and marketing campaigns really are and which marketing techniques worked best. Maintaining a uniform reporting system will help to increase revenues and margins by eliminating errors in the sales process. From ready-to-use forms, you can easily process inquiries, track sales leads, maintain mailing lists, and manage callbacks. C.G.T. Canadian Legal Forms sales and marketing forms let you:

- Enter and update leads (contacts, clients, customers, vendors, etc.)
- Maintain important information about leads: the people involved (originator, caller, company representative, etc.), relevant dates (date opened, due date, etc.), materials sent, as well as the probability for successful follow-up.
- Keep relevant notes regarding the leads.
- Review the history of a lead, so you have a record of who did what and when.
- Perform statistical analysis of your data, and analyze sales trends.

Personnel

Under the broad umbrella of personnel management falls scheduling, payroll and record keeping. Whether you have one or several dozen employees, keeping track of when they work, how much they get paid, or when they are absent, injured or sick can be a time-consuming task. *Business Forms* can help ease your burden.

These forms enable you to record an employee's history with the company, make changes to an employee's file or salary record or verify the accuracy of information you have on an employee. Keep track of employee turnover and projected personnel needs with the *Employee Record Change* and *Vacation Request*. Document your temporary employment needs.

Setting schedules was never easier with the *Employee Weekly Time Record* and *Work Overtime Report*. Additional forms help you accurately and objectively evaluate job applicants and job performance, as well as track company property loaned out to employees.

You'll have what you need to manage and maintain your employee records with the comprehensive index of basic personnel forms.

ABSENCE REQUEST

Employee: _____ Date: _____

Department: _____

Date(s) Requested: From _____ To _____

Hour(s) Requested: From _____ To _____

       With Pay ( )   Without Pay ( )   Make Up ( )

Reason For Absence: _____

_____

_____

_____

_____

_____

_____

_____

       Approved ( )   Not Approved ( )

Supervisor Remarks: _____

_____

_____

_____

_____

_____

_____

_____   _____
Employee Signature   Date

_____   _____
Supervisor Signature   Date Approved

1

ACCOUNTS RECEIVABLE AGING

Date:

Account Name	Balance	Current Balance	30-60 days	60-90 days	Over 90 days

Totals:

ACCOUNTS RECEIVABLE SUMMARY

Customer Number	Customer Name	Balance Forward	Month of	Month of	Month of	New Balance	Previous Items	
							Date	Amount

ACKNOWLEDGEMENT OF TERMS ON INITIAL STOCKING ORDER

Date:

To:

We are pleased that we can furnish you with an initial stocking order on the following credit terms:

1. Credit on the initial order shall not exceed $.

2. You shall pay as follows:

3. You shall secure this credit line as follows:

4. Future invoices shall be paid according to our customary trade terms.

5. Your total credit line (including your initial order) is $.

6. Other terms:

If this meets with your understanding, please sign below and return. We thank you for your business.

Very truly,

_____

Acknowledged:

_____
Customer

ACTIVITY COMPLETIONS THIS WEEK

WEEK OF:

S	M	T	W	T	F	S	ACTIVITY	DATE NEEDED	FOLLOW-UP	FOLLOW-UP DATE	✓

ADVERTISING BUDGET

For The Year: _____

Company Name: _____

Month	Radio	Television	Newspaper	Other	Monthly Cost
January:	_____	_____	_____	_____	_____
February:	_____	_____	_____	_____	_____
March:	_____	_____	_____	_____	_____
April:	_____	_____	_____	_____	_____
May:	_____	_____	_____	_____	_____
June:	_____	_____	_____	_____	_____
July:	_____	_____	_____	_____	_____
August:	_____	_____	_____	_____	_____
September:	_____	_____	_____	_____	_____
October:	_____	_____	_____	_____	_____
November:	_____	_____	_____	_____	_____
December:	_____	_____	_____	_____	_____

Total Yearly Advertising Cost: $ _____

ADVERTISING RECORD

Item Advertised	Date(s) Ad Aired/ Published	Advertising Medium	Number of Respondents	Sales Results
_____	_____	_____	_____	_____
_____	_____	_____	_____	_____
_____	_____	_____	_____	_____
_____	_____	_____	_____	_____
_____	_____	_____	_____	_____
_____	_____	_____	_____	_____
_____	_____	_____	_____	_____
_____	_____	_____	_____	_____
_____	_____	_____	_____	_____
_____	_____	_____	_____	_____
_____	_____	_____	_____	_____
_____	_____	_____	_____	_____
_____	_____	_____	_____	_____
_____	_____	_____	_____	_____
_____	_____	_____	_____	_____
_____	_____	_____	_____	_____
_____	_____	_____	_____	_____
_____	_____	_____	_____	_____
_____	_____	_____	_____	_____
_____	_____	_____	_____	_____
_____	_____	_____	_____	_____
_____	_____	_____	_____	_____

AGENDA

DATE: _____ TIME: _____ LOCATION: _____

PURPOSE: _____

ATTENDEES: _____

_____

SCHEDULE:

Time	
8:00 — 8:30	
8:30 — 9:00	
9:00 — 9:30	
9:30 — 10:00	
10:00 — 10:30	
10:30 — 11:00	
11:00 — 11:30	
11:30 — 12:00	
12:00 — 12:30	
12:30 — 1:00	
1:00 — 1:30	
1:30 — 2:00	
2:00 — 2:30	
2:30 — 3:00	
3:00 — 3:30	
3:30 — 4:00	
4:00 — 4:30	
4:30 — 5:00	
5:00 — 5:30	
5:30 — 6:00	
6:00 — 6:30	
6:30 — 7:00	
7:00 — 7:30	
7:30 — 8:00	
8:00 — 8:30	
8:30 — 9:00	

ANNUAL ATTENDANCE RECORD
FOR CALENDAR YEAR _____

Employee: _____   Social Insurance No.: _____

Position: _____   Department: _____

Day	Jan	Feb	Mar	Apr	May	June	July	Aug	Sept	Oct	Nov	Dec
1												
2												
3												
4												
5												
6												
7												
8												
9												
10												
11												
12												
13												
14												
15												
16												
17												
18												
19												
20												
21												
22												
23												
24												
25												
26												
27												
28												
29												
30												
31												

A = Absent	O = Other	H = Holiday	P = Personal Leave Approved
S = Sick	T = Tardy	F = Funeral Leave	U = Unauthorized Absence
J = Jury Duty	I = Job Injury	V = Vacation	L = Leave of Absence

Comments and summary of attendance: _____

_____

ANNUAL BUDGET
For the Year of _____

FIXED ANNUAL EXPENSES:	ESTIMATE	ACTUAL	DIFFERENCE	DIFFERENCE in + OR - %
Mortgages	$_____	$_____	$_____	_____
Loans	$_____	$_____	$_____	_____
Rents	$_____	$_____	$_____	_____
Insurance	$_____	$_____	$_____	_____
Estimated Taxes	$_____	$_____	$_____	_____
Total Fixed Monthly Expenses	$_____	$_____	$_____	_____

VARIABLE (controllable) ANNUAL EXPENSES:

Telephone	$_____	$_____	$_____	_____
Gas & electricity	$_____	$_____	$_____	_____
Accounts payable	$_____	$_____	$_____	_____
Travel & entertainment	$_____	$_____	$_____	_____
Vehicle fuel & maintenance	$_____	$_____	$_____	_____
Laundry & cleaning	$_____	$_____	$_____	_____
Dues & subscriptions	$_____	$_____	$_____	_____
Wages	$_____	$_____	$_____	_____
Payroll taxes	$_____	$_____	$_____	_____
Commissions	$_____	$_____	$_____	_____
Office supplies	$_____	$_____	$_____	_____
Postage	$_____	$_____	$_____	_____
Other expenses	$_____	$_____	$_____	_____
Total Variable Expense	$_____	$_____	$_____	_____

TOTAL ANNUAL EXPENSE

Annual Income	$_____	$_____	$_____	_____
Less: Annual expenses	$_____	$_____	$_____	_____

TOTAL ANNUAL INCOME BEFORE TAXES $_____

ANNUAL EXPENSE COMPARISON/PROJECTION

Name: _____ Year: _____

INCOME	Last Year	This Year	Next Year
Salaries	$ _____	$ _____	$ _____
Commissions/Bonuses	_____	_____	_____
Interest	_____	_____	_____
Alimony	_____	_____	_____
Child Support	_____	_____	_____
Rent	_____	_____	_____
Property Sales	_____	_____	_____
Royalties	_____	_____	_____
Security Sales	_____	_____	_____
Trust Fund	_____	_____	_____
Annuities	_____	_____	_____
Pensions	_____	_____	_____
_____	_____	_____	_____
Total Income	$ _____	$ _____	$ _____
TAXES			
Property Taxes	$ _____	$ _____	$ _____
Employment Insurance	_____	_____	_____
Provincial/City Income Tax	_____	_____	_____
Federal Income Tax	_____	_____	_____
Canada Pension Plan	_____	_____	_____
Total Tax Expenditures	$ _____	$ _____	$ _____
LIVING EXPENSES			
Mortgage/Rent	$ _____	$ _____	$ _____
Food	_____	_____	_____
Utilities: Electric	_____	_____	_____
Heat	_____	_____	_____
Water	_____	_____	_____
Phone	_____	_____	_____
Other: _____	_____	_____	_____
_____	_____	_____	_____
Credit Cards:_____	_____	_____	_____
_____	_____	_____	_____
Insurance: Health	_____	_____	_____
Life	_____	_____	_____
Auto	_____	_____	_____
Loans: _____	_____	_____	_____
_____	_____	_____	_____
Personal/Health Care	_____	_____	_____
Clothing/Maint.	_____	_____	_____
Child Care	_____	_____	_____
Education	_____	_____	_____
Home Maintenance	_____	_____	_____
Membership Fees	_____	_____	_____
Entertainment/Rec.	_____	_____	_____
Contributions	_____	_____	_____
Investments	_____	_____	_____
Savings	_____	_____	_____
Auto: Maintenance	_____	_____	_____
Loan	_____	_____	_____
Gas	_____	_____	_____
Legal Expenses	_____	_____	_____
Other: _____	_____	_____	_____
_____	_____	_____	_____
Total Living Expenses	$ _____	$ _____	$ _____

APPLICANT INTERVIEW SCHEDULE

Date _____

Appointment Time	Name of Applicant	Position Applied For	Comments	Recommendation

APPLICANT RATING

APPLICANT:

POSITION/DEPARTMENT:

INTERVIEWED BY: DATE:

JOB REQUIREMENTS	EXCELLENT	GOOD	FAIR	POOR	N/A
_____	_____	_____	_____	_____	_____
_____	_____	_____	_____	_____	_____
_____	_____	_____	_____	_____	_____
_____	_____	_____	_____	_____	_____
_____	_____	_____	_____	_____	_____
_____	_____	_____	_____	_____	_____
_____	_____	_____	_____	_____	_____
_____	_____	_____	_____	_____	_____
_____	_____	_____	_____	_____	_____
_____	_____	_____	_____	_____	_____
_____	_____	_____	_____	_____	_____
_____	_____	_____	_____	_____	_____
_____	_____	_____	_____	_____	_____

GENERAL COMMENTS / OVERALL APPRAISAL _____

_____

_____

_____

_____

_____

_____

RECOMMENDATION: HIRE ❑   REJECT ❑   OTHER ❑ _____

APPLICATION FOR EMPLOYMENT

PERSONAL INFORMATION

DATE

NAME   SOC. INS. NO.

PRESENT ADDRESS

PERMANENT ADDRESS

PHONE NO.   REFERRED BY

EMPLOYMENT DESIRED

POSITION   DATE AVAILABLE   SALARY REQ.

ARE YOU EMPLOYED?   IF SO, MAY WE INQUIRE OF YOUR PRESENT EMPLOYER

EVER APPLIED TO THIS COMPANY?   WHERE?   WHEN?

EDUCATION

	NAME AND LOCATION OF SCHOOL	*YEARS ATTENDED	*DATE GRADUATED	AREA OF STUDY
HIGH SCHOOL				
COLLEGE				
TRADE OR BUSINESS SCHOOL				
GRADUATE/PROFESSIONAL SCHOOL				

GENERAL

SUBJECTS OF SPECIAL STUDY OR RESEARCH WORK

WHAT FOREIGN LANGUAGES DO YOU SPEAK FLUENTLY?   READ   WRITE

MILITARY SERVICE   RANK

SPECIAL QUESTIONS

DO NOT ANSWER **ANY** OF THE QUESTIONS IN THIS FRAMED AREA UNLESS THE EMPLOYER HAS **CHECKED A BOX PRECEDING** A QUESTION, THEREBY INDICATING THAT THE INFORMATION IS REQUIRED FOR A BONA FIDE OCCUPATION-AL QUALIFICATION, IS DICTATED BY NATIONAL SECURITY LAWS, OR IS NEEDED FOR OTHER LEGALLY PERMISSIBLE REASONS.

❑ HEIGHT_____FEET_____INCHES   ❑ CITIZEN OF CANADA_____YES_____NO

❑ WEIGHT_____LBS.   ❑ DATE OF BIRTH*_____

❑ _____

PHYSICAL RECORD

DO YOU HAVE ANY PHYSICAL DEFECTS THAT PRECLUDE YOU FROM
PERFORMING ANY WORK FOR WHICH YOU ARE BEING CONSIDERED?

WERE YOU EVER INJURED?   GIVE DETAILS:

HAVE YOU ANY DEFECTS IN HEARING?   IN VISION?   IN SPEECH?

IN CASE OF EMERGENCY, NOTIFY

FORMER EMPLOYERS

(LIST BELOW YOUR LAST FOUR EMPLOYERS, STARTING WITH THE LAST ONE FIRST.)

DATE (MONTH/YEAR)	NAME AND ADDRESS OF EMPLOYER	SALARY	POSITION	REASON FOR LEAVING
FROM TO				
FROM TO				
FROM TO				
FROM TO				

REFERENCES

NAME   ADDRESS   BUSINESS   YEARS KNOWN

1

2

3

I AUTHORIZE INVESTIGATION OF ALL STATEMENTS CONTAINED IN THIS APPLICATION. I UNDERSTAND THAT MISREPRESEN-
TATION OR OMISSION OF FACTS CALLED FOR IS CAUSE FOR DISMISSAL. FURTHER, I UNDERSTAND AND AGREE THAT MY
EMPLOYMENT IS FOR NO DEFINITE PERIOD AND MAY, REGARDLESS OF THE DATE OF PAYMENT OF MY WAGES AND SALARY,
BE TERMINATED AT ANY TIME WITHOUT ANY PREVIOUS NOTICE.

DATE   SIGNATURE

INTERVIEWED BY   DATE

· DO NOT WRITE BELOW THIS LINE ·

REMARKS

APPEARANCE		CHARACTER	
PERSONALITY		ABILITY	

HIRED   FOR DEPT.   POSITION   WILL REPORT   SALARY/WAGES

APPROVED: 1.   2.   3.

EMPLOYMENT MANAGER   DEPT. HEAD   GENERAL MANAGER

THIS FORM HAS BEEN DESIGNED TO COMPLY WITH PROVINCIAL AND FEDERAL FAIR EMPLOYMENT PRACTICE LAWS PRO-
HIBITING DISCRIMINATION ON THE BASIS OF AN APPLICANT'S SEX OR MINORITY STATUS. QUESTIONS DIRECTLY OR INDI-
RECTLY REFLECTING SUCH STATUS HAVE BEEN INCLUDED ONLY WHERE NEEDED TO DETERMINE A BONA FIDE OCCUPA-
TIONAL QUALIFICATION OR FOR OTHER PERMISSIBLE PURPOSES. SUCH QUESTIONS ARE APPROPRIATELY NOTED ON THE
APPLICATION. NOTWITHSTANDING THESE EFFORTS, THE MANUFACTURER OF THIS FORM ASSUMES NO RESPONSIBILITY,
AND HEREBY DISCLAIMS ANY LIABILITY FOR INCLUSION IN THIS FORM, OF ANY QUESTIONS UPON WHICH A VIOLATION OF
PROVINCIAL AND FEDERAL FAIR EMPLOYMENT PRACTICE LAWS MAY BE BASED.

APPLICATION—UPDATE

We appreciate your continuing interest in our company. In order to reactivate your application for 30 additional days, please complete the following information.

Full Name: _____

Social Insurance No.: _____

Home Telephone Number: _____

Date of Previous Application: _____

Position Applying For: _____

Information to be Added: _____

_____

_____

_____

_____

_____

_____

_____   _____
            Signature   Date

Only edit your application for positions that you are currently available and for which you are qualified. Otherwise your application will not be considered.

APPOINTMENT SCHEDULE

Day: _____

	APPOINTMENT	NOTES
7:00		
7:15		
7:30		
7:45		
8:00		
8:15		
8:30		
8:45		
9:00		
9:15		
9:30		
9:45		
10:00		
10:15		
10:30		
10:45		
11:00		
11:15		
11:30		
11:45		
12:00		
12:15		
12:30		
12:45		
1:00		
1:15		
1:30		
1:45		
2:00		
2:15		
2:30		
2:45		
3:00		
3:15		
3:30		
3:45		
4:00		
4:15		
4:30		
4:45		
5:00		
5:15		
5:30		
5:45		
6:00		
6:15		
6:30		
6:45		

ATTENDANCE RECORD

WEEK STARTING:	HOURS						
	SUN	MON	TUE	WED	THU	FRI	SAT

BACKORDER LOG

From _____ To _____

DATE OF ORDER	STOCK NUMBER	ITEM	TOTAL ON ORDER	TOTAL BACK-ORDERED	DIFFER-ENCE	SHIP DATE	CANCEL DATE	INI-TIALS

BANK COMPARISON WORKSHEET

Key Considerations	Need or expected monthly income	BANK 1	BANK 2	BANK 3
Types of services offered				
Checking				
Savings				
Investments				
Federal Tax Deposits				
Small Business Counselling				
Loans/Lines of Credit				
Pension Administration				
Business Credit Cards				
Fees				
Checking Account				
Monthly Fee				
Minimum Balance				
Per Check Charge				
Interest Paid				
Other				
Savings Account				
Interest Rate				
Minimum Balance				
Transaction Fee				
Other				
Credit Card Processing				
Monthly Fee				
Discount Rate (fee)				
Other				
Other Factors				
Convenient Location				
Existing Relationship				
Interest in Small Business				

BANK RECONCILIATION WORKSHEET

For the Month of _____

	Beginning Balance	Debit	Credit		Ending Balance
Bank Balance as of	_____				
Outstanding Checks:	_____	_____	_____	_____	_____
	_____	_____	_____		_____
	_____	_____	_____		_____
	_____	_____	_____		_____
	_____	_____	_____		_____
	_____	_____	_____		_____
	_____	_____	_____		_____
	_____	_____	_____	_____	_____
Outstanding Deposits:	_____	_____		_____	_____
	_____	_____		_____	_____
	_____	_____		_____	_____
	_____	_____		_____	_____
	_____	_____		_____	_____
Adjustments:	_____	_____		_____	_____
Totals	_____	_____	_____	_____	
Adjusted Bank Balance					$ _____
Ledger Balance as of	_____				
Outstanding Checks:	_____	_____		_____	_____
	_____	_____		_____	_____
	_____	_____		_____	_____
	_____	_____		_____	_____
	_____	_____		_____	_____
	_____	_____		_____	_____
	_____	_____		_____	_____
	_____	_____		_____	_____
Outstanding Deposits:	_____	_____	_____		_____
	_____	_____	_____		_____
	_____	_____	_____		_____
Adjustments:	_____	_____	_____		_____
	_____	_____	_____		_____
Totals	_____	_____	_____	_____	

Adjusted General Ledger Balance must agree with Adjusted Bank Balance. $ _____

Prepared by _____ Date _____

Approved by _____ Date _____

BENEFITS PLANNING CHECKLIST

	Date	Company Policy ✔	Competitor Policy ✔	Employee Preference	Recommendation
Retirement Plan					
Deferred Compensation					
Incentive Stock Option					
Disability Insurance					
Health Insurance					
Group Life Insurance					
Dental Insurance					
Education Benefits					
Profit-Sharing					
Performance Bonus					
Scholarship Aid					
Relocation Expense					
Group Legal					
Wage Continuation					
Child Care					
Club Memberships					
Stock Purchase Plan					
Paid-Up Annuities					
Low-Interest Loans					
Company Car					
Financial Counseling					
Sabbaticals					

BI-WEEKLY PLANNING SCHEDULE

SUNDAY	MONDAY	TUESDAY	WEDNESDAY	THURSDAY	FRIDAY	SATURDAY

SUNDAY	MONDAY	TUESDAY	WEDNESDAY	THURSDAY	FRIDAY	SATURDAY

BI-WEEKLY TRACKING SCHEDULE

1											
2											
3											
4											
5											
6											
7											
8											
9											
10											
11											
12											
13											
14											
15											

BREAK-EVEN ANALYSIS

	Fixed Costs	Controllable Costs
Product costs		
Average cost of product	$ _____	$_____
Monthly selling expenses		
Sales salaries and commissions	$ _____	$_____
Advertising	$ _____	$_____
Miscellaneous selling expense	$ _____	$_____
Monthly general expense		
Office salaries	$ _____	$_____
Supplies	$ _____	$_____
Miscellaneous general expense	$ _____	$_____
Totals	$ _____	$_____
Number of units produced	_____	
Average selling price per unit	$ _____	
Results		
Contribution margin per unit	$ _____	
Monthly unit sales at break-even point	$ _____	
Monthly sales dollars at break-even point	$ _____	

CALLER'S PHONE LOG

Name of Caller:

Call Date	Access Code	Company/Person Called			Area Code	Phone Number	Total Time
		Name	City	Prov			

CASH REGISTER BALANCE SHEET

Employee _____

Shift/Hours _____ Today's Date _____

		RECEIPTS AND MEMOS:
Cash To Start		
Opening - F/S		
Register Reading		
Extra Cash		
Rebates		
TOTAL		
$100		
$50		
$20		
$10		
$5		
$1		
Dollars (Change)		
.50		
.25		
.10		
.05		
.01		
Checks		
Ending Cash		
Ending - F/S		
- Payouts		
+ Credit Cards		
Deposits		
Refunds		
TOTAL		
AMOUNT OVER (+)		
AMOUNT SHORT (—)		

CASH REPORT

DATE _____

CHECKS OUT		
TOTAL		

CASH OUT		
TOTAL		

RECEIPTS		
CHECKS		
CASH		
CREDIT CARDS		
TOTAL ALL RECEIPTS		
- CASH PAID OUT		
+ CASH TO START		
BALANCE		
OVER OR SHORT		
MEMOS:		
BANK DEPOSIT		

ACCOUNT #	
DEPOSIT DATE	
DEPOSITED BY	
SIGNATURE	

CHARGE ACCOUNT PAYMENT RECORD

From: _____   To: _____

Date	To	For	Charge To Account #	Amount Paid
_____	_____	_____	_____	_____
_____	_____	_____	_____	_____
_____	_____	_____	_____	_____
_____	_____	_____	_____	_____
_____	_____	_____	_____	_____
_____	_____	_____	_____	_____
_____	_____	_____	_____	_____
_____	_____	_____	_____	_____
_____	_____	_____	_____	_____
_____	_____	_____	_____	_____
_____	_____	_____	_____	_____
_____	_____	_____	_____	_____
_____	_____	_____	_____	_____
_____	_____	_____	_____	_____
_____	_____	_____	_____	_____
_____	_____	_____	_____	_____
_____	_____	_____	_____	_____
_____	_____	_____	_____	_____
_____	_____	_____	_____	_____
_____	_____	_____	_____	_____
_____	_____	_____	_____	_____
_____	_____	_____	_____	_____
_____	_____	_____	_____	_____
_____	_____	_____	_____	_____
_____	_____	_____	_____	_____
_____	_____	_____	_____	_____
_____	_____	_____	_____	_____
_____	_____	_____	_____	_____
_____	_____	_____	_____	_____

CLIENT BILLING/TIME SUMMARY

HOUR	CLIENT	ACTIVITY	TIME	
			HRS.	MIN.

CLIENT'S RECORD OF CHARGES

	PERSON	HOURLY CHARGES	HOURS	TOTAL	PAID	BALANCE DUE
7:00						
7:15						
7:30						
7:45						
8:00						
8:15						
8:30						
8:45						
9:00						
9:15						
9:30						
9:45						
10:00						
10:15						
10:30						
10:45						
11:00						
11:15						
11:30						
11:45						
12:00						
12:15						
12:30						
12:45						
1:00						
1:15						
1:30						
1:45						
2:00						
2:15						
2:30						
2:45						
3:00						
3:15						
3:30						
3:45						
4:00						
4:15						
4:30						
4:45						
5:00						
5:15						
5:30						
5:45						
6:00						
6:15						
6:30						
6:45						
7:00						

COLLECTION REPORT

Date:

Customer Name:_____ Acct. No.:_____

Street: _____

City: _____ Province: _____ Postal Code: _____

Phone: _____ Contact: _____

Period ending: _____

Account Status:

Current Balance $ _____

30 days $ _____

60 days $ _____

Over 90 Days $ _____

Agreement for payments?

Compliance?

Recommended Action:

_____   Continue credit

_____   Stop credit and negotiate payment plan

_____   Stop credit and collect

_____   Other

By: _____

COMMERCIAL CREDIT APPLICATION

T NAME_____ **F** NAME_____

O ADDRESS _____ **R** ADDRESS _____

CITY/PROVINCE/P.C._____ **O** CITY/PROVINCE/P.C. _____

CREDIT MANAGER_____ **M** _____

PHONE NUMBER _____ PHONE NUMBER_____

BUSINESS: ❑ SOLE PROPRIETORSHIP ❑ PARTNERSHIP ❑ CORPORATION

NUMBER OF YEARS IN BUSINESS _____ D AND B NUMBER _____

...ME AND ADDRESS OF INDIVIDUALS OR PARTNERS: NAME/TITLE/PHONE NO. OF CORPORATE OFFICERS

_____

_____

_____

_____

...ME OF PERSON TO CONTACT REGARDING P.O.s AND PAYMENTS, TITLE, ADDRESS AND PHONE NUMBER

_____ _____

_____ _____

_____ _____

_____ _____

...NK REFERENCE, BANK ACCOUNT NUMBER, CONTACT, TITLE AND PHONE NUMBER

_____ _____

_____ _____

_____ _____

_____ _____

...ADE REFERENCES: COMPANY NAME, ADDRESS, CONTACT AND TITLE, AND PHONE NUMBER

_____ _____ _____

_____ _____ _____

_____ _____ _____

_____ _____ _____

I DO HEREBY CERTIFY THE ABOVE   SIGNED _____
INFORMATION TO BE TRUE TO THE   TITLE _____
BEST OF MY KNOWLEDGE   DATE _____

COMMERCIAL CREDIT APPLICATION

Date: _____

Corporate name: _____

Type of organization: _____

Trade name (if different): _____

Address:_____

City: _____ Province:_____ Postal Code:_____

Owner/Manager:_____Business Phone:_____

How long in business?_____D & B Rated:_____

Credit line requested: $ _____ Credit Terms: _____

Bank References:

Name _____ Branch _____ Acct. No. _____

Name _____ Branch _____ Acct. No. _____

Trade References:

Name _____ Address _____

Name _____ Address _____

Name _____ Address _____

Name _____ Address _____

Pending lawsuits against company:

_____

_____

_____

Are financial statements available? _____

     The undersigned authorizes credit inquiries. We further acknowledge that any credit privileges may be withdrawn at any time. I certify the above information to be true and accurate.

_____

COMMITTEE / ORGANIZATION MEMBERS

COMMITTEE NAME: DATE:
PURPOSE:
SPECIFIC GOALS:
HEAD OF COMMITTEE:

POSITION	NAME	ADDRESS	PHONE

CONSENT TO RELEASE INFORMATION

Date:

To: _____ Employee

From:

A request to verify employment information has been received by us from:

_____

Which information may we release?

_____ Salary

_____ Position

_____ Department

_____ Supervisor

_____ Employment dates

_____ Part-time/full-time

_____ Whether you work under a maiden name

_____ Wage garnishes, if any

_____ Reason for separation

_____ Other _____

_____   _____
Submitted by   Approved by

PLEASE RETURN THIS FORM AS SOON AS POSSIBLE SO WE MAY QUICKLY RESPOND TO THE REQUEST.

CONSUMER CREDIT APPLICATION

Date:_____

Name:_____ Soc. Ins. No.:_____

Address:_____

City:_____ Province:_____ Postal Code: _____

Resident since:_____ Monthly Rent/Mortgage Payment: _____

Employed by:_____ Position: _____

Employed since:_____ Salary: $ _____

Spouse's name:_____ Number of dependents:_____

Additional income sources:

_____ $ _____

_____ $ _____

Outstanding financial obligations:

_____ $ _____

_____ $ _____

Pending lawsuits: _____

Have you filed bankruptcy within last 10 years? _____

Credit References:

Name _____ Address _____

Name _____ Address _____

Name _____ Address _____

Bank References:

Bank name:_____ Address:_____

Checking Acct. No.:_____ Savings Acct. No.: _____

Visa Card:_____ Master Card:_____

American Express: _____ Other Credit Cards:_____

    I certify the above information to be true and accurate.

_____
Applicant Signature

CREDIT CHANGE NOTICE

Date:

To: Credit Department

Sales Personnel

Customer File

New credit terms/limits are effective immediately for the following account:

Customer Name: _____

Address: _____

City: _____ Province: _____ Postal Code: _____

Account No.:_____ New Account: _____

Current Account: _____

Renewed Account: _____

Sales Representative _____

New credit limit: $

Changed from prior limit of: $

Other terms:

Agreement on prior balance:

By: _____

CREDIT HISTORY

NAME OF APPLICANT _____ SPOUSE'S NAME _____

ADDRESS _____

_____

TELEPHONE _____ FAX NUMBER _____

BUSINESS NAME _____ BUSINESS NAME _____

BUSINESS ADDRESS _____ BUSINESS ADDRESS _____

_____   _____

BUSINESS TELEPHONE _____ BUSINESS TELEPHONE _____

DATE APPROVED	CREDIT LINE	PAYMENT DUE		PAYMENT RECEIVED		BALANCE DUE	DATE OF 1ST NOTICE	DATE OF 2ND NOTICE
		AMOUNT	DATE	AMOUNT	DATE			

COLLECTION AGENT   DATE OF ATTORNEY REFERRAL

DISPOSITION

CREDIT INFORMATION CHECKLIST

Customer: _____

Address: _____

City: _____ Province:_____ Postal Code:_____

Telephone No.:_____ Contact: _____

Date of Order or Credit Request: _____

Sales Representative: _____

	Date Requested	Date Received	Date Approved
Credit Application	_____	_____	_____
Financial Statements	_____	_____	_____
Inspection Report	_____	_____	_____
Bank Reference	_____	_____	_____
Trade References:			
_____	_____	_____	_____
_____	_____	_____	_____
_____	_____	_____	_____
Sales Report	_____	_____	_____
D & B Report	_____	_____	_____
Other Credit Reports:			
_____	_____	_____	_____
_____	_____	_____	_____
Guarantor's Financials	_____	_____	_____
Lien/Security Check	_____	_____	_____
Insurance Verification	_____	_____	_____
Other:			
_____	_____	_____	_____

CREDIT LOG

From: _____ To: _____

Account Identification #	Name of Account	Date Account Was Opened	Maximum Credit	Current Credit Available	Difference	Current	30	60	90
TOTAL									

41

CREDIT MEMO

SOLD TO

SHIPPED TO

TERMS:

REASON FOR CREDIT	
APPROVED BY	APPROVED BY
DATE	DATE

YOUR ORDER NO.	ORDER DATE	OUR ORDER NO.

ITEM	QTY.	INVOICE NO./DESCRIPTION	UNIT PRICE	AMOUNT

CREDIT MEMO

CREDIT MEMO ISSUED DATE	TOTAL CREDIT

42

CREDIT POLICY

1.   Procedures for Approving Credit:

2.   Standard Credit Terms:

3.   Account Review Procedures:

4.   Collection Procedures:

Exceptions to this Credit Policy <u>must</u> be approved by the credit manager.

CRITICAL EVENTS LOG

DATE	EVENT	CPOMMENTS

CUMULATIVE BUDGET

	Jan.	Feb.	Mar.	April	May	June	July	Aug.	Sept.	Oct.	Nov.	Dec.	Cumu-lative
Cash – begin balance													
Cash – cont. operations													
Total cash available													
Less:													
Capital expenditures													
Interest paid													
Dividends paid													
Debt retired													
Other													
Total cash disbursements													
Cash balance or deficit													
Add:													
Short-term loans													
Long-term loans													
Capital stock issued													
Cash balance – ending													

45

CUSTOMER CREDIT ANALYSIS

Customer:_____ Date:_____

Address:_____ Phone:_____

City: _____ Province:_____ Postal Code:_____

Account No.: _____

D & B Rating:_____

Other Credit Ratings:_____

_____

	Excellent	Good	Fair	Poor
Bank Reference:	_____	_____	_____	_____
_____				
Credit Reference:	_____	_____	_____	_____
_____				
Credit Reference:	_____	_____	_____	_____
_____				
Credit Reference:	_____	_____	_____	_____
_____				
Credit Report:	_____	_____	_____	_____
_____				
Credit Report:	_____	_____	_____	_____
_____				
Other:	_____	_____	_____	_____

FINANCIAL ANALYSIS SUMMARY

Balance Sheet:	_____	_____	_____	_____
Income Statement:	_____	_____	_____	_____

SUMMARY:

Credit Recommended:_____

Credit Approved: _____

CUSTOMER FINANCIAL ANALYSIS

Customer: _____

Account No.: _____ Date: _____

Address: _____

City: _____ Province: _____ Postal Code: _____

| This Period | ANALYSIS | Last Period |

Date: _____,_____(year).   Date: _____,_____(year).

_____Current Ratio_____

_____Profit/Sales _____

_____Profit/Net Worth _____

_____Profit/Net Working Capital _____

_____Sales/Inventory_____

_____Current Debt/Net Worth _____

_____Total Debt/Net Worth _____

_____Sales to Receivables _____

_____Total Secured Debt _____

_____Total Tangible Assets _____

Summary:

Recommendations:

CUSTOMER INVOICE

From _____   Invoice # _____

Address _____   Invoice Date _____

_____   Phone _____

To _____   Ship to _____

Address _____   Address _____

_____   _____

_____   _____

Phone _____   Phone _____

Quantity	Unit	Item #	Price	Discount	Extended Price
_____	_____	_____	_____.___	_____.___	_____.___
_____	_____	_____	_____.___	_____.___	_____.___
_____	_____	_____	_____.___	_____.___	_____.___
_____	_____	_____	_____.___	_____.___	_____.___
_____	_____	_____	_____.___	_____.___	_____.___
_____	_____	_____	_____.___	_____.___	_____.___
_____	_____	_____	_____.___	_____.___	_____.___
_____	_____	_____	_____.___	_____.___	_____.___
_____	_____	_____	_____.___	_____.___	_____.___
_____	_____	_____	_____.___	_____.___	_____.___
_____	_____	_____	_____.___	_____.___	_____.___
_____	_____	_____	_____.___	_____.___	_____.___
_____	_____	_____	_____.___	_____.___	_____.___
_____	_____	_____	_____.___	_____.___	_____.___
_____	_____	_____	_____.___	_____.___	_____.___

Taxable Sale $_____.___

Nontaxable Sale $_____.___

Total Sale $_____.___

Sales Tax $_____.___

Other $_____.___

Balance Due $_____.___

Thank You!

CUSTOMER LIST

CUSTOMER	BILL TO ADDRESS	SHIPPING ADDRESS	CUSTOMER CATEGORY	PRICE CODE	CREDIT LIMIT

CUSTOMER STATEMENT

From _____ Phone _____

Address _____

_____

To _____ Phone _____

Address _____

_____

Statement Date _____ Statement # _____ Customer # _____ Page # _____

Reference	Date	Code	Description	Amount	Balance
_____	_____	_____	_____	_____.__	_____.__
_____	_____	_____	_____	_____.__	_____.__
_____	_____	_____	_____	_____.__	_____.__
_____	_____	_____	_____	_____.__	_____.__
_____	_____	_____	_____	_____.__	_____.__
_____	_____	_____	_____	_____.__	_____.__
_____	_____	_____	_____	_____.__	_____.__
_____	_____	_____	_____	_____.__	_____.__
_____	_____	_____	_____	_____.__	_____.__
_____	_____	_____	_____	_____.__	_____.__
_____	_____	_____	_____	_____.__	_____.__

Codes: C = Credit Memo   P = Payment   A = Discount Allowed

D = Debit Memo   I = Invoice   F = Finance Charge   TOTAL DUE $ _____ .

Please return with your remittance.

Customer Name _____ Phone _____

Address _____

_____

Statement Date _____ Statement Number _____

Customer Number _____ Statement Total _____

Amount Remitted _____

50

DAILY ACTIVITY PLANNER AND APPOINTMENT SCHEDULE

DATE:			
TO DO FROM YESTERDAY	✓		**SCHEDULE**
		6:00	
		6:30	
		7:00	
		7:30	
		8:00	
TO DO TODAY	✓	8:30	
		9:00	
		9:30	
		10:00	
		10:30	
		11:00	
		11:30	
		12:00	
		12:30	
		1:00	
		1:30	
		2:00	
		2:30	
		3:00	
		3:30	
		4:00	
		4:30	
FOLLOW-UP	✓	5:00	
		5:30	
		6:00	
		6:30	
		7:00	
		7:30	
DO TOMORROW			**COMMENTS**

DAILY CASH RECONCILIATION

DATE:

CASH ON HAND	$ _____	
CASH SALES	$ _____	
CASH SALES – C.O.D.	$ _____	
COLLECTIONS	$ _____	
LESS: Deposits	$ _____	
_____	$ _____	
BALANCE		$ _____

CASH	$ _____	
CHECKS	$ _____	
CASH PAYOUTS	$ _____	
OUT TICKETS	$ _____	
_____	$ _____	
BALANCE		$ _____

NOTES:

DAILY JOB LOG

DATE _____

Job Begins	Job Ends	Date	% Job Complete	Job Address	Nature of Work	# Hours on Job

_____
Signature of Employee

53

DAILY ORGANIZER

	DATE:	
DO FROM YESTERDAY		✓

APPOINTMENTS TODAY		✓

PHONE CALLS TO MAKE	✓	**REMINDERS AND NOTES**	✓

DAILY PRODUCTION RECORD

PRODUCT CENTER: _____   SHIFT: _____   DATE: _____

SCHEDULE				PRODUCTION					
ORDER NO.	CUSTOMER	PRODUCT NAME AND SIZE	QUANTITY ORDERED	START	STOP	TOTAL HOURS	WEIGHT CHARGED	PRODUCT WEIGHT

DELAYS		REASON FOR DELAY
BEGAN	ENDED	

PREPARER: _____   APPROVED BY: _____

55

DAILY SALES JOURNAL

	Today's Date	Taxable Product Sales	Sales tax	Non-Taxable Sales	Shipping	Total Sales	Comments
Month _____ Year _____							
1							
2							
3							
4							
5							
6							
7							
8							
9							
10							
11							
12							
13							
14							
15							
16							
17							
18							
19							
20							
21							
22							
23							
24							
25							
26							
27							
28							
29							
30							
31							
TOTALS							

DAILY TASK LIST

DATE: _____

| ✔ | MEET WITH: |

| ✔ | CALL/FAX/E-MAIL: |

| ✔ | WRITE: |

DAILY TIME SHEET

Shift _____ Employee's Name _____ Date _____

Job or Function	Began Work	End Work	Authorized Overtime	Comments and Recommendations

Approved By _____

58

| SOLD TO | | **DEBIT MEMO** |
| | | |

TERMS:

| REASON FOR DEBIT |
| |

| SHIPPED TO | |
| | |

| APPROVED BY | APPROVED BY |
| DATE | DATE |

| YOUR ORDER NO. | ORDER DATE | OUR ORDER NO. |

ITEM	QTY.	INVOICE NO./DESCRIPTION	UNIT PRICE	AMOUNT

DEBIT MEMO

DEBIT MEMO ISSUED DATE	TOTAL DEBIT AMOUNT

DEBTS / PAID-OUTSTANDING

Creditor's Name				
Type of Debt				
Account #				
Telephone #				
Opening Balance				
Current Interest Rate				
January				
Payment				
Interest/Fees				
New Balance				
February				
Payment				
Interest/Fees				
New Balance				
March				
Payment				
Interest/Fees				
New Balance				
April				
Payment				
Interest/Fees				
New Balance				
May				
Payment				
Interest/Fees				
New Balance				
June				
Payment				
Interest/Fees				
New Balance				
July				
Payment				
Interest/Fees				
New Balance				
August				
Payment				
Interest/Fees				
New Balance				
September				
Payment				
Interest/Fees				
New Balance				
October				
Payment				
Interest/Fees				
New Balance				
November				
Payment				
Interest/Fees				
New Balance				
December				
Payment				
Interest/Fees				
New Balance				

DEPARTMENT OVERTIME REQUEST

Department:_____ Date:_____

Employee	Employee ID No.	Overtime Requested	Authorized
	Total		

Signature: _____

61

DEPARTMENT PAYROLL

Period beginning: _____ Ending: _____

Employee	Hours		Pay Rate	Wages		Total Wages
	Reg	OT		Reg	OT	
TOTALS						

DEPARTMENTAL OBJECTIVES

Department: _____   Supervisor: _____

Date: _____

OBJECTIVE	ASSIGNED EMPLOYEE	DUTIES ASSIGNED	DUE DATE
_____	_____	_____	_____
_____	_____	_____	_____
_____	_____	_____	_____
_____	_____	_____	_____
_____	_____	_____	_____
_____	_____	_____	_____
_____	_____	_____	_____
_____	_____	_____	_____
_____	_____	_____	_____
_____	_____	_____	_____
_____	_____	_____	_____
_____	_____	_____	_____
_____	_____	_____	_____
_____	_____	_____	_____
_____	_____	_____	_____

DEPRECIATION SCHEDULE

For the Year of _____

Description	Purchase Date	Life	Method	Cost Basis	Prior Depreciation	Current Depreciation	Net Book Value
_____	__/__/__	____	____	_____.__	_____.__	_____.__	_____.__
_____	__/__/__	____	____	_____.__	_____.__	_____.__	_____.__
_____	__/__/__	____	____	_____.__	_____.__	_____.__	_____.__
_____	__/__/__	____	____	_____.__	_____.__	_____.__	_____.__
_____	__/__/__	____	____	_____.__	_____.__	_____.__	_____.__
_____	__/__/__	____	____	_____.__	_____.__	_____.__	_____.__
_____	__/__/__	____	____	_____.__	_____.__	_____.__	_____.__
_____	__/__/__	____	____	_____.__	_____.__	_____.__	_____.__
_____	__/__/__	____	____	_____.__	_____.__	_____.__	_____.__
_____	__/__/__	____	____	_____.__	_____.__	_____.__	_____.__
_____	__/__/__	____	____	_____.__	_____.__	_____.__	_____.__
_____	__/__/__	____	____	_____.__	_____.__	_____.__	_____.__
_____	__/__/__	____	____	_____.__	_____.__	_____.__	_____.__
_____	__/__/__	____	____	_____.__	_____.__	_____.__	_____.__
_____	__/__/__	____	____	_____.__	_____.__	_____.__	_____.__
_____	__/__/__	____	____	_____.__	_____.__	_____.__	_____.__
_____	__/__/__	____	____	_____.__	_____.__	_____.__	_____.__
_____	__/__/__	____	____	_____.__	_____.__	_____.__	_____.__
_____	__/__/__	____	____	_____.__	_____.__	_____.__	_____.__
_____	__/__/__	____	____	_____.__	_____.__	_____.__	_____.__
_____	__/__/__	____	____	_____.__	_____.__	_____.__	_____.__
_____	__/__/__	____	____	_____.__	_____.__	_____.__	_____.__
_____	__/__/__	____	____	_____.__	_____.__	_____.__	_____.__
_____	__/__/__	____	____	_____.__	_____.__	_____.__	_____.__

TOTALS   _____.__ _____.__ _____.__

For general ledger use straight line method. For other uses be advised by a tax consultant on which method to use.

Prepared by _____ Date _____

Approved by _____ Date _____

DIARY

Date	

DIRECT MAIL ANALYSIS

NAME OF PROMOTION _____   DATE _____

PRODUCT		PROMOTION	
SELLING PRICE		CIRCULARS	
ADD: SERVICE CHARGE		INSERTS	
TOTAL SELLING PRICE		LETTERS	
LESS: MERCHANDISE COST		ENVELOPES	
SHIPPING/DELIVERY		ORDER FORMS	
ORDER PROCESSING		LIST RENTAL	
COST OF RETURNS		INSERTING	
BAD DEBT		ADDRESSING	
		MAILING	
		POSTAGE	
		MISCELLANEOUS	
		TOTAL CIRCULATION COST	
		ADD: FIXED OVERHEAD PER M	
TOTAL COST		TOTAL COST (C)	
UNIT PROFIT *		BREAK EVEN SALES PER M**	

NET PROFIT

FORECASTED NET SALES PER M (In Units)	
LESS: BREAK EVEN SALES ** (In Units)	–
UNIT SALES PER M EARNING TOTAL PROFIT	
UNIT PROFIT*	x
NET PROFIT PER M	$
M CIRCULARS MAILED	x
TOTAL NET PROFIT	

PREPARED BY _____

DISCIPLINARY REPORT

Employee Name	Date	Department

Statement of Problem

Date of Offense	Location	Time

Reported By	Title	Department

Witnesses

Comments

Supervisor's Signature	Employee's Signature

Prior Warnings	Date of Last Warning

Summary of Corrective Action To Be Taken

Recommendations

The above offense(s) have been noted and recorded in the employee's personnel file.

EMPLOYEE BENEFITS ANALYSIS

	Company Contribution	Employee Contribution	Benefit Total Cost (Annual)
Retirement Plan	$	$	$
Deferred Compensation	$	$	$
Incentive Stock Option	$	$	$
Disability Insurance	$	$	$
Health Insurance	$	$	$
Group Life Insurance	$	$	$
Dental Insurance	$	$	$
Education Benefits	$	$	$
Profit-Sharing	$	$	$
Performance Bonus	$	$	$
Scholarship Aid	$	$	$
Relocation Expense	$	$	$
Group Legal	$	$	$
Wage Continuation	$	$	$
Child Care	$	$	$
Club Memberships	$	$	$
Stock Purchase Plan	$	$	$
Paid-Up Annuities	$	$	$
Low-Interest Loans	$	$	$
Company Car	$	$	$
Financial Counseling	$	$	$
Sabbaticals	$	$	$
	$	$	$
	$	$	$

EMPLOYEE CHECKOUT RECORD

Employee Name _____   Department _____

Termination Date _____

Complete or return each
of the below checked items
upon termination.

<table>
<tr><th>RETURN</th><th>COMPLETE</th></tr>
<tr><td>❑ Air Travel Cards</td><td>❑ Confidentiality Report</td></tr>
<tr><td>❑ Catalog / Sales Items</td><td>❑ Exit Interview</td></tr>
<tr><td>❑ Company Documents</td><td>❑ Expense Reports</td></tr>
<tr><td>❑ Company Tools</td><td>❑ Termination Forms</td></tr>
<tr><td>❑ Credit Cards.</td><td>❑ Other:</td></tr>
<tr><td>❑ Customer Lists</td><td>❑ _____</td></tr>
<tr><td>❑ Expense Accounts</td><td>❑ _____</td></tr>
<tr><td>❑ Identification Badge</td><td>❑ _____</td></tr>
<tr><td>❑ Keys to Premises</td><td>❑ _____</td></tr>
<tr><td>❑ Petty Cash Advances</td><td>❑ _____</td></tr>
<tr><td>❑ Sample Products</td><td></td></tr>
<tr><td>❑ Security Statement</td><td></td></tr>
<tr><td>❑ Vehicle(s)</td><td></td></tr>
<tr><td>❑ Other Items:</td><td></td></tr>
<tr><td>❑ _____</td><td></td></tr>
<tr><td>❑ _____</td><td></td></tr>
<tr><td>❑ _____</td><td></td></tr>
<tr><td>❑ _____</td><td></td></tr>
<tr><td>❑ _____</td><td></td></tr>
</table>

_____
Supervisor

EMPLOYEE EVALUATION CHECKLIST

Name of Employee _____ Date _____

Department _____ Last Evaluation Date _____

Reviewer _____ Title _____

	Excellent	Good	Fair	Poor
Honesty	_____	_____	_____	_____
Productivity	_____	_____	_____	_____
Technical Skills	_____	_____	_____	_____
Quality of Work	_____	_____	_____	_____
Consistency of Work	_____	_____	_____	_____
Enthusiasm	_____	_____	_____	_____
Cooperation	_____	_____	_____	_____
Attitude	_____	_____	_____	_____
Initiative	_____	_____	_____	_____
Relations with others	_____	_____	_____	_____
Originality	_____	_____	_____	_____
Punctuality	_____	_____	_____	_____
Attendance	_____	_____	_____	_____
Reliability	_____	_____	_____	_____
Appearance	_____	_____	_____	_____
Creativity	_____	_____	_____	_____
Other:				
_____	_____	_____	_____	_____
_____	_____	_____	_____	_____
_____	_____	_____	_____	_____

Comments:

_____
Signature and Title of Reviewer

EMPLOYEE EXIT INTERVIEW

Employee: _____ Position: _____

Department: _____ Supervisor: _____

Employed From: _____ To: _____

Reason For Termination: _____

Employee Returned:

_____ keys   _____ safety equipment   _____ tools

_____ ID card   _____ company documents   _____ uniform

_____ credit card   _____ other company property   _____ company vehicle

Employee was informed about restrictions on:

_____ trade secrets   _____ removing company documents

_____ patents   _____ employment with competitor (if applicable)

_____ other_____

Employee exit questions/answers:

1. Did management adequately recognize your contributions? _____

_____

2. Did you feel that you had the support of management? _____

_____

3. Were you properly trained for your job? _____

_____

4. Was your work rewarding? _____

_____

5. Were you fairly treated by the company? _____

_____

6. Was your salary adequate?_____

_____

7. How were your working conditions? _____

_____

8. Were you supervised properly? _____

_____

9. Did you understand all company policies? _____

_____

10. Have you seen theft of company property?_____

_____

11. How can the company improve security? _____

_____

12. How can the company improve working conditions?_____

_____

13. What do you feel are the company's strengths? _____

_____

14. What do you feel are the company's weaknesses? _____

_____

15. Other employee comments or suggestions:_____

_____

EMPLOYEE RECORD CHANGE

Employee: Date:

Department/Section: No.:

Effective Date:

Pay Rate Change:

From _____ To _____

Job Title Change:

From _____ To _____

Job Classification Change:

From _____ To _____

Shift Change:

From _____ To _____

Full-Time/Part-Time Change:

From _____ To _____

Temporary/Permanent Change:

From _____ To _____

Other:

_____   _____

_____   _____

_____   _____

              Submitted by   Approved by

EMPLOYEE SALARY RECORD

Employee: _____

Starting Date: _____ Starting Salary: _____

POSITION	INCREASE DATE	INCREASE	TYPE OF INCREASE (MERIT/PROMOTION, etc.)

EMPLOYEE SELF-EVALUATION

CONFIDENTIAL

Payroll No.	Name of Employee	Supervisor	Date

List your most successful accomplishments since your last performance evaluation:

1. _____

2. _____

3. _____

4. _____

List your least successful accomplishments since your last performance evaluation:

1. _____

2. _____

3. _____

4. _____

List your area(s) of greatest strength:

1. _____

2. _____

3. _____

4. _____

List your areas where you need most improvement:

1. _____

2. _____

3. _____

4. _____

What can you do to effect improvement:

1. _____

2. _____

3. _____

4. _____

What can the company do:

1. _____

2. _____

3. _____

4. _____

EMPLOYEE TURNOVER LOG

Department					Year		

Current		Prior Months			Cumulative Year to Date		
Month	Total # Employees	Employees Added	Employees Terminated	Turnover + or −	Employees Added	Employees Terminated	Turnover + or −
ANNUAL TOTALS							

Comments:

Submitted by: Approved by:

EMPLOYEE WEEKLY TIME RECORD

WEEK ENDING:

Employee	Mon	Tues	Wed	Thurs	Fri	Sat	Sun	Total	Gross Pay	Ded.	Net Pay

EMPLOYMENT RECORD

Employee: _____

Employee Number: _____

Date	Department	Position	Rate	Per	Comments

Submitted by: _____ Date: _____

Approved by: _____ Date: _____

EMPLOYMENT REFERENCE RESPONSE FORM

Name of Employee:_____

Dates of Service: _____/_____ to _____/_____

Position at Terrmination: _____

Reason for Termination: _____

NOTE: When asked to supply an employment reference, this company only provides short responses. This report is used for all employees. The lack of any further information should not be interpreted as either a favorable or unfavorable reference.

Submitted by:_____ Title: _____

Date: _____ Company: _____

EQUIPMENT ASSIGNMENT SCHEDULE

	Date			
Employee	Function/Operation	Machine	From	To

EQUIPMENT REPAIR REQUEST

Dept.:   Date:

Type Equip.:   Mach. No.:

Maintenance/Repair Required:

Signature: _____

Maintenance Report

Name:

Repair/Maintenance:

Comments:

EQUIPMENT SERVICE LOG

Dept:

Location:

Machine No.:

REPAIR DATE	REPAIRS OR MAINTENANCE	PROBLEM/CAUSE	REPAIRED BY	NEXT INSPECTION DUE

EQUIPMENT SERVICE RECORD

ITEM

MODEL   SERIAL NUMBER   I.D. NUMBER

PURCHASE DATE   VALUE AT PURCHASE   CONDITION AT PURCHASE

VENDOR

LEASED FROM   LENGTH OF LEASE   RATE

CONDITION OF ITEM (DESCRIBE)

SERVICE CONTRACT WITH   PHONE

DATE	TIME	SERVICE PERFORMED	PARTS NEEDED	APPROVED

EXPENSE BUDGET

	Month Ending:			Year to Date		
	Estimate	Actual	Difference	Estimate	Actual	Difference
FIXED EXPENSES						
Exec. salaries..........................						
Office salaries.........................						
Payroll taxes..........................						
Pensions & benefits.................						
Travel and entertainment.........						
Executive fees & expenses.......						
Insurance						
Rent						
Depreciation						
Taxes....................................						
Legal....................................						
Audit.....................................						
Telephone and fax						
Utilities.................................						
Contributions.........................						
Postage						
Dues.....................................						
Other....................................						
VARIABLE EXPENSES						
Office salaries.........................						
Pensions & benefits.................						
Payroll taxes..........................						
Travel and entertainment.........						
Telephone and fax						
Office supplies.......................						
Bad debts..............................						
Postage						
Contributions.........................						
Other....................................						
TOTAL						

EXPENSE LOG

EMPLOYEE _____ WEEK ENDING _____ DEPT. _____

	SUNDAY	MONDAY	TUESDAY	WEDNESDAY	THURSDAY	FRIDAY	SATURDAY	WEEKLY TOTAL
FROM								
TO								
TO								
TOTAL AUTO MILES								
MILEAGE (MI.)								
GAS–OIL–LUBE								
PARKING & TOLLS								
AUTO RENTAL								
LOCAL–CAB/LIMO								
AIR–RAIL–BUS								
LODGING								
BREAKFAST								
LUNCH								
DINNER								
LAUNDRY								
PHONE, ETC.								
TIPS								
OTHER								
ENTERTAINMENT*								
TOTAL PER DAY								

*ENTERTAINMENT

DATE	ITEM	PERSONS ENTERTAINED	BUSINESS RELATIONSHIP	AT	PURPOSE	AMOUNT

PURPOSE OF TRIP _____

_____

REMARKS _____

DATE _____

SIGNATURE _____

SUMMARY

TOTAL EXPENSES	
LESS CASH ADVANCED	
LESS CHARGES TO CO.	
AMOUNT DUE ❑ ME	
❑ CO.	

FACILITY PLANNER

By answering the questions below, you can determine the requirements for your ideal business location:

What kind of facility does your business need?

❑ Home   ❑ Office   ❑ Store

❑ Factory   ❑ Warehouse   ❑ Other

Do you intend to lease or purchase your business facility? _____

How many square feet do you need? _____

What special requirements does your business have?

❑ Electrical _____   ❑ Plumbing _____

❑ Heating _____   ❑ Air Conditioning _____

❑ Ventilation _____   ❑ Refrigeration _____

❑ Water _____   ❑ Storage _____

❑ Access _____   ❑ Other _____

Rank the following (from 1-5) in terms of importance to your business.

_____ Customer Convenience

_____ Supplier Proximity

_____ Employee Proximity

_____ Competitor Proximity

_____ Personal Preference

Where could you locate your business to satisfy the two most important considerations listed above?

_____

_____

_____

_____

15 MINUTE APPOINTMENT SCHEDULE

DAY:_____ DATE: _____

	APPOINTMENT	NOTES
7:00		
7:15		
7:30		
7:45		
8:00		
8:15		
8:30		
8:45		
9:00		
9:15		
9:30		
9:45		
10:00		
10:15		
10:30		
10:45		
11:00		
11:15		
11:30		
11:45		
12:00		
12:15		
12:30		
12:45		
1:00		
1:15		
1:30		
1:45		
2:00		
2:15		
2:30		
2:45		
3:00		
3:15		
3:30		
3:45		
4:00		
4:15		
4:30		
4:45		
5:00		
5:15		
5:30		
5:45		
6:00		
6:15		
6:30		
6:45		

FIRST WARNING NOTICE

Employee _____ Employee No. _____

Shift _____ Time_____ a.m.   Date of
                                           p.m.   Warning _____

Date of Violation _____

Time of Violation _____

Location of Violation _____

NATURE OF VIOLATION

❑ Substandard Work   ❑ Improper Conduct   ❑ Lateness

❑ Carelessness   ❑ Disobedience/   ❑ Absenteeism
                          Insubordination

❑ Clocking Out Early   ❑ Clocking Out Wrong   ❑ Intoxication/Drugs/
                                                  Drinking

❑ Other _____

SUPERVISOR COMMENTS

_____

_____

_____

_____

_____

_____

EMPLOYEE COMMENTS

_____

_____

_____

_____

Signatures

_____   _____   _____
        Employee   Supervisor   Date

5 DAY ACTIVITIES SCHEDULE

MONDAY	✓			✓
1. _____	❑	6.	_____	❑
2. _____	❑	7.	_____	❑
3. _____	❑	8.	_____	❑
4. _____	❑	9.	_____	❑
5. _____	❑	10.	_____	❑

TUESDAY	✓			✓
1. _____	❑	6.	_____	❑
2. _____	❑	7.	_____	❑
3. _____	❑	8.	_____	❑
4. _____	❑	9.	_____	❑
5. _____	❑	10.	_____	❑

WEDNESDAY	✓			✓
1. _____	❑	6.	_____	❑
2. _____	❑	7.	_____	❑
3. _____	❑	8.	_____	❑
4. _____	❑	9.	_____	❑
5. _____	❑	10.	_____	❑

THURSDAY	✓			✓
1. _____	❑	6.	_____	❑
2. _____	❑	7.	_____	❑
3. _____	❑	8.	_____	❑
4. _____	❑	9.	_____	❑
5. _____	❑	10.	_____	❑

FRIDAY	✓			✓
1. _____	❑	6.	_____	❑
2. _____	❑	7.	_____	❑
3. _____	❑	8.	_____	❑
4. _____	❑	9.	_____	❑
5. _____	❑	10.	_____	❑

5 DAY PLANNER

MON	TUE	WED	THU	FRI

4-YEAR FINANCIAL TRENDS

PRIMARY INDICATORS				
INCOME DATA				
NET SALES				
COST OF GOODS SOLD				
GROSS PROFIT				
NET PROFIT BEFORE TAXES				
NET PROFIT AFTER TAXES				
ASSETS – LIABILITIES				
ACCOUNTS RECEIVABLE				
INVENTORY				
TOTAL ASSETS				
ACCOUNTS PAYABLE				
DEBT – SHORT-TERM				
DEBT – LONG-TERM				
TOTAL LIABILITIES				
NET WORTH				
RATIOS ANALYSIS				
CURRENT				
TOTAL DEBT TO TOTAL ASSETS				
COLLECTION PERIOD				
NET SALES TO INVENTORY				
NET PROFIT MARGIN AFTER TAXES				
RETURN ON NET WORTH				

GENERAL LEDGER

ACCOUNT / I.D. # _____

ACCOUNT NAME _____

ADDRESS _____

CONTACT _____

TEL. _____

SHEET NO. _____ OF _____

DATE	DESCRIPTION	CHARGES	CREDITS	BALANCE	
				CHARGES	CREDITS
	Amount Forward				

GOALS THIS QUARTER

For Quarter Beginning:

Priority	Goal	Name	Project #	Completed (✓)	Date Completed

UNCOMPLETED PROJECTS

Project	Assigned To	Scheduled Completion Date

HOURLY CHARGE SHEET

HOUR	SERVICE RENDERED	HRS.	MIN.

HOURLY WORK SCHEDULE

Name: _____

Employer: _____

Location: _____

Salary/Hr.: _____

Hours Worked:

Week of:	Sun.	Mon.	Tue.	Wed.	Thur.	Fri.	Sat.	Total Hours	Total Pay	Date Paid
	____	____	____	____	____	____	____	____	____	____
	____	____	____	____	____	____	____	____	____	____
	____	____	____	____	____	____	____	____	____	____
	____	____	____	____	____	____	____	____	____	____
	____	____	____	____	____	____	____	____	____	____
	____	____	____	____	____	____	____	____	____	____
	____	____	____	____	____	____	____	____	____	____
	____	____	____	____	____	____	____	____	____	____
	____	____	____	____	____	____	____	____	____	____
	____	____	____	____	____	____	____	____	____	____
	____	____	____	____	____	____	____	____	____	____
	____	____	____	____	____	____	____	____	____	____
	____	____	____	____	____	____	____	____	____	____
	____	____	____	____	____	____	____	____	____	____
	____	____	____	____	____	____	____	____	____	____
	____	____	____	____	____	____	____	____	____	____
	____	____	____	____	____	____	____	____	____	____

INCIDENT / GRIEVANCE REPORT

Date of Report _____

Name of Employee _____

Department or Payroll No. _____

Date of Incident / Grievance _____

1. Describe Incident / Grievance _____

_____

_____

_____

2. Actions Taken _____

_____

_____

_____

3. Witnesses:

Name	Title	Address / Dept. / Payroll No.
_____	_____	_____
_____	_____	_____
_____	_____	_____
_____	_____	_____

4. Reported To:

Person	Date and Department
_____	_____
_____	_____
_____	_____
_____	_____

_____

Completed By

USE REVERSE IF YOU
NEED ADDITIONAL SPACE

96

INSURANCE WORKSHEET

COVERAGES	AMOUNT	COST	COMMENTS
Building			
Structure			
Fire	_____	_____	_____
Windstorm	_____	_____	_____
Lightning	_____	_____	_____
Vandalism	_____	_____	_____
Earthquake	_____	_____	_____
Trees, plants, and shrubs	_____	_____	_____
Glass Coverage	_____	_____	_____
Exterior Signs	_____	_____	_____
Total	_____	_____	_____
Property			
Inventory			
Base Level	_____	_____	_____
Peak Season (+25-40%)	_____	_____	_____
Employee Pilferage	_____	_____	_____
Robbery and Burglary	_____	_____	_____
Money and Securities	_____	_____	_____
Accounts Receivable	_____	_____	_____
Valuable Papers	_____	_____	_____
Boiler and Machinery	_____	_____	_____
Personal Effects	_____	_____	_____
Automobile(s)	_____	_____	_____
Total	_____	_____	_____
Operations			
General Business Liability			
Bodily Injury to Others	_____	_____	_____
Damage to Property of Others	_____	_____	_____
Personal Injury to Others	_____	_____	_____
Professional Liability	_____	_____	_____
Key Person	_____	_____	_____
Loss of Income			
Direct	_____	_____	_____
Indirect	_____	_____	_____
Extra Expenses Following Loss	_____	_____	_____
Loss of Refrigeration	_____	_____	_____
Total	_____	_____	_____
Other			
Medical (owner/employees)	_____	_____	_____
Disability (owner/employees)	_____	_____	_____
Worker's Compensation	_____	_____	_____
Life (owner/employees)	_____	_____	_____
Total	_____	_____	_____
Total Insurance Package		_____	_____

INVENTORY

DATE: _____

ITEM	QTY.	UNIT PRICE	EXTENSION	ITEM	QTY.	UNIT PRICE	EXTENSIO
						SUB-TOTAL	
						TOTAL	

INVENTORY CONTROL

USAGE RECORD FOR: DATE:

DEPARTMENT:

Item	Description	Retail	Sold Last Season	On Hand	Qty. On Order	Qty. To Order	Total	Current Units	Units Sold	Notes

INVENTORY SCHEDULE

❏ RETAIL   ❏ WHOLESALE   FROM: TO:

PRODUCT	PRICE (RETAIL)	QUANTITY	% DISCOUNT	NET UNIT PRICE

INVOICE

SOLD TO _____   DATE _____

_____   TERMS _____

SHIP TO _____   INVOICE NO. _____

_____   ORDER NO. _____

_____   DEPT. _____

SHIP VIA _____   SALES PERSON _____

QUANTITY	ITEM NO.	DESCRIPTION	PRICE	TOTAL

INVOICE CONTROL LOG

Month: _____

Page _____ of _____

INVOICE DATE	NO.	ACCOUNTS PAYABLE	DESCRIPTION	GENERAL ACCOUNT NAME	NO.	AMOUNT	DATE PAID	CHECK NO.

JOB DESCRIPTION

Job Title   _____

Grade   _____

Pay Range   _____

Reports To   _____

Job Class   _____

Location   _____

Department   _____

Job Summary   _____

_____

_____

_____

Work Performed   _____

_____

_____

_____

_____

_____

_____

_____

Experience Required   _____

_____

_____

_____

_____

_____

Skilled Required   _____

_____

_____

_____

Prepared by   _____ Date _____

Approved by   _____ Date _____

LAYAWAY ORDER

Sold To: _____   Date: _____

_____   Sold By: _____

_____   Picked Up ❏   Delivered ❏

Item	Stock No.	Quantity Ordered	Unit Price	Total Amount

Payment Plan: Total   _____

No of Payments _____   Sales Tax   _____

$_____ per Payment   Total Due   _____

$_____ Final Payment   On Deposit   _____

                                        Balance   _____

LONG DISTANCE PHONE CALL RECORD

Date	Name of Caller	Party Called	Number Called	Time from - to

MACHINE RUN REPORT

Machine			Date	
Time Started	Time Stopped	Activity		By

MAILING LIST UPDATE

	DATE ADDED	NUMBER	CUSTOMER NAME	CUSTOMER ADDRESS	MAILING SENT	RECOMMENDATION	
						MAINTAIN	DROP
1							
2							
3							
4							
5							
6							
7							
8							
9							
10							
11							
12							
13							
14							
15							
16							
17							
18							
19							
20							
21							
22							
23							
24							
25							

MEDICAL LOG

Period Ending _____

Date	Time	Employee Name	Attended by	Injury / Illness	Treatment

Recommendations:

MEMO

REFER TO:
❑ YOUR ❑ MY ❑ BELOW ❑ ATTACHED
❑ LETTER ❑ PHONE CALL ❑ ORDER ❑ _____
❑ INQUIRY ❑ MEMO ❑ FAX ❑ TELEGRAM
❑ E-MAIL DATED:_____

TO

FROM

SIGNATURE/TITLE/LOCATION/PHONE/FAX/DATE

REPLY

SIGNATURE/TITLE/LOCATION/PHONE/FAX/DATE

MILEAGE REIMBURSEMENT REPORT

Employee: _____

Driver's License No.: _____ Registration No.: _____

Type of Vehicle: _____

Department: _____ Month: _____

Total mileage this month: _____ @ $0._____ Per Mile = $_____

_____   _____
Approved By   Date

_____
Title

MONTH BY DAYS

	✔	
SUNDAY		
MONDAY		
TUESDAY		
WEDNESDAY		
THURSDAY		
FRIDAY		
SATURDAY		
SUNDAY		
MONDAY		
TUESDAY		
WEDNESDAY		
THURSDAY		
FRIDAY		
SATURDAY		
SUNDAY		
MONDAY		
TUESDAY		
WEDNESDAY		
THURSDAY		
FRIDAY		
SATURDAY		
SUNDAY		
MONDAY		
TUESDAY		
WEDNESDAY		
THURSDAY		
FRIDAY		
SATURDAY		
SUNDAY		
MONDAY		
TUESDAY		
WEDNESDAY		
THURSDAY		
FRIDAY		
SATURDAY		

MONTHLY / ANNUAL RECORD OF CREDIT CARD PURCHASES

JANUARY		FEBRUARY		MARCH		APRIL		MAY		JUNE	
CYCLE END DATE _____		CYCLE END DATE _____		CYCLE END DATE _____		CYCLE END DATE _____		CYCLE END DATE _____		CYCLE END DATE _____	
ITEM	COST	ITEM	COST	ITEM	COST	ITEM	COST	ITEM	COST	ITEM	COST
TOTAL		TOTAL		TOTAL		TOTAL		TOTAL		TOTAL	

MONTHLY / ANNUAL RECORD OF CREDIT CARD PURCHASES

JULY		AUGUST		SEPTEMBER		OCTOBER		NOVEMBER		DECEMBER	
CYCLE END DATE _____		CYCLE END DATE _____		CYCLE END DATE _____		CYCLE END DATE _____		CYCLE END DATE _____		CYCLE END DATE _____	
ITEM	COST	ITEM	COST	ITEM	COST	ITEM	COST	ITEM	COST	ITEM	COST
TOTAL		TOTAL		TOTAL		TOTAL		TOTAL		TOTAL	

MONTHLY ACCOUNT ANALYSIS

Date:

Customer Name:_____

Account No: _____ Phone: _____

Address: _____

City: _____ Province:_____ Postal Code:_____

Current Month	Orders on hand	Prior Month
$	Current	$
$	30-60	$
$	60-90	$
$	Over 90	$
_____		_____
$	**Total Balance** $	

Purchases to date this year: $

Purchases to date last year: $

Collection period: This year: _____

Last year: _____

Credit Line: $

Present Balance: $

Amount (over) or under: $

Present credit terms:

Agreement to reduce balance?

Compliance with agreement:

Recommended action:

By: _____

MONTHLY ACTIVITY REVIEW

MONTH:

DATE	ASSIGNED TO	ACTIVITY OR PROJECT	INITIAL DATE	REVISED DATE	FOLLOW-UP	✓

DATE OF LAST REVIEW/UPDATE	DATE OF NEXT REVIEW/UPDATE

MONTHLY BUDGET

For the Month of _____

FIXED MONTHLY EXPENSES:	ESTIMATE	ACTUAL	DIFFERENCE	DIFFERENCE in + OR - %
Mortgages	$_____	$_____	$_____	$_____
Loans	$_____	$_____	$_____	$_____
Rents	$_____	$_____	$_____	$_____
Insurance	$_____	$_____	$_____	$_____
Estimated Taxes	$_____	$_____	$_____	$_____
Total Fixed Monthly Expenses	$_____	$_____	$_____	$_____

VARIABLE (controllable) MONTHLY EXPENSES:

	ESTIMATE	ACTUAL	DIFFERENCE	DIFFERENCE
Telephone	$_____	$_____	$_____	$_____
Gas & electricity	$_____	$_____	$_____	$_____
Accounts payable	$_____	$_____	$_____	$_____
Travel & entertainment	$_____	$_____	$_____	$_____
Vehicle fuel & maintenance	$_____	$_____	$_____	$_____
Laundry & cleaning	$_____	$_____	$_____	$_____
Dues & subscriptions	$_____	$_____	$_____	$_____
Wages	$_____	$_____	$_____	$_____
Payroll taxes	$_____	$_____	$_____	$_____
Commissions	$_____	$_____	$_____	$_____
Office supplies	$_____	$_____	$_____	$_____
Postage	$_____	$_____	$_____	$_____
Other expenses	$_____	$_____	$_____	$_____
Total Variable Expense	$_____	$_____	$_____	$_____

TOTAL MONTHLY EXPENSE

Monthly Income	$_____	$_____	$_____	$_____
Less: Monthly expenses	$_____	$_____	$_____	$_____

TOTAL NET MONTHLY INCOME BEFORE TAXES

$_____

MONTHLY CHECKLIST

Year:	J	F	M	A	M	J	J	A	S	O	N	D

MONTHLY PRODUCT SALES TREND

YEAR: _____

	$ LAST YEAR	$ GOAL THIS YR	% CHANGE	$ LAST YEAR	$ GOAL THIS YR	% CHANGE	$ LAST YEAR	$ GOAL THIS YR	% CHANGE	$ LAST YEAR	$ GOAL THIS YR	% CHANGE	TOTAL $ LAST YEAR	$ GOAL THIS YR	% CHANGE
JAN															
FEB															
MAR															
APR															
MAY															
JUN															
JUL															
AUG															
SEP															
OCT															
NOV															
DEC															
TOTAL															

PREPARED BY: _____

DATE: _____

MONTHLY SALES ANALYSIS

MONTH	$ LAST YEAR	$ GOAL THIS YR	$ ACTUAL THIS YR	%	$ LAST YEAR	$ GOAL THIS YR	$ ACTUAL THIS YR	%	TOTAL $ LAST YEAR	$ GOAL THIS YR	$ ACTUAL THIS YR	%
JAN												
FEB												
MAR												
APR												
MAY												
JUN												
JUL												
AUG												
SEP												
OCT												
NOV												
DEC												
YEARLY TOTALS												

PREPARED BY:

MONTHLY SUMMARY

1					
2					
3					
4					
5					
6					
7					
8					
9					
10					
11					
12					
13					
14					
15					
16					
17					
18					
19					
20					
21					
22					
23					
24					
25					
26					
27					
28					
29					
30					
31					

MONTHLY SUMMARY

										✔
1										
2										
3										
4										
5										
6										
7										
8										
9										
10										
11										
12										
13										
14										
15										
16										
17										
18										
19										
20										
21										
22										
23										
24										
25										
26										
27										
28										
29										
30										
31										

NEW ACCOUNT CREDIT APPROVAL

Customer:_____

Address:_____

City: _____ Province:_____ Postal Code:_____

Phone:_____ Contact:_____

Sales Representative:_____ Date:_____

Credit Line: $ _____

Shipment Terms:

Payment Terms:

Initial Order Terms:

Other Terms:

Credit Review By:

Approved By: _____

NEW HIRE APPROVAL REQUEST

Request No. _____ Date _____

Name of Applicant _____

Job Position _____

_____

_____

❏ Part Time   ❏ Full Time   ❏ Permanent   ❏ Temporary   ❏ Shift

Starting Salary $_____

Immediate Supervisor _____ Tel. No. & Ext. _____

Reason For Hire _____ New Position _____

Department _____ Location _____

Job Duties _____

_____

_____

_____

_____

Relocation Authorization _____

_____

Special Instructions _____

_____

_____

Starting Date _____

_____
Requested By

123

NOTICE OF DISMISSAL

Date

To:

We regret to notify you that your employment with the company shall be terminated on
,   , for the following reasons:

Severance pay shall be in accordance with company policy. Insurance benefits shall continue in accordance with applicable laws and/or the provisions of our employee policy. Please contact
, at your earliest convenience, who will arrange other termination matters with you.

We truly regret this action is necessary.

Sincerely,

Copies to:

NOTICE OF DISPATCH

Date:

To:

On   ,   (year), you placed an order with us for the following
goods:

Your order will be sent via   (carrier) and should arrive on
or about   ,   (year).

Upon delivery, please have C.O.D. payment ready in the amount of $, by:

_____ cash, certified or bank check, or money order

_____ personal check

Thank you for your order, and we look forward to your continued patronage.

Very truly,

_____

NOTICE OF INCORRECT CREDIT DEDUCTION

Date:

To:

Thank you for your recent payment. However, we note you have deducted a credit of $

Unfortunately, we cannot agree to this credit because:

Accordingly, we shall debit your account by said amount. Please notify us if you have any questions.

We appreciate your patronage and your understanding.

Very truly,

_____

NOTICE OF MEETING

Meeting group _____   Date _____

Type of meeting _____   Starting time _____

Called by _____   Location _____

Purpose _____

Please bring with you _____

Meeting goals _____

Chairperson _____

Recorder _____

Agenda items

1) _____

2) _____

3) _____

4) _____

5) _____

6) _____

7) _____

8) _____

9) _____

10) _____

NOTICE TO STOP GOODS IN TRANSIT

Date:

To: _____
           (Common Carrier)

You have our goods in transit for delivery to:

_____

_____

_____

This is to confirm our previous telephoned or telegraphed instruction to stop delivery of these goods. Please return said goods to us; we shall pay return freight charges.

No negotiable bill of lading or document of title has been delivered to our customer (consignee).

A copy of our shipping documents for these goods is enclosed for your convenience.

Very truly,

_____

Copy to:

_____
Customer

ONE-YEAR PROJECT COMPLETION TRACKING

PROJECT:

Completion Phase	Assigned To	12 months from commencement											

ONE-YEAR CHECKLIST

YEAR										
JANUARY										
FEBRUARY										
MARCH										
APRIL										
MAY										
JUNE										
JULY										
AUGUST										
SEPTEMBER										
OCTOBER										
NOVEMBER										
DECEMBER										

OUT OF STOCK NOTICE

Date: _____ Order no.: _____ Order date: _____

To: _____

_____

_____

Item number	Description	Quantity	Price

Your order cannot be completed because we are temporarily out of stock on the above. Please return this completed form. We apologize for any inconvenience.

Estimated shipping date: _____   Please return form to: _____

❑ Back order — ship as soon as possible   _____

❑ Substitute (specify) _____   _____

❑ Cancel   _____

Signed (customer): _____   _____

OUTSTANDING BILLS RECORD

Name: _____ Date: _____

Pay To	Date Due	Amount Due	Date Paid	Amount Paid
_____	_____	$ _____	_____	$ _____
_____	_____	$ _____	_____	$ _____
_____	_____	$ _____	_____	$ _____
_____	_____	$ _____	_____	$ _____
_____	_____	$ _____	_____	$ _____
_____	_____	$ _____	_____	$ _____
_____	_____	$ _____	_____	$ _____
_____	_____	$ _____	_____	$ _____
_____	_____	$ _____	_____	$ _____
_____	_____	$ _____	_____	$ _____
_____	_____	$ _____	_____	$ _____
_____	_____	$ _____	_____	$ _____
_____	_____	$ _____	_____	$ _____
_____	_____	$ _____	_____	$ _____
_____	_____	$ _____	_____	$ _____
_____	_____	$ _____	_____	$ _____
_____	_____	$ _____	_____	$ _____
_____	_____	$ _____	_____	$ _____
_____	_____	$ _____	_____	$ _____
_____	_____	$ _____	_____	$ _____
_____	_____	$ _____	_____	$ _____
_____	_____	$ _____	_____	$ _____
_____	_____	$ _____	_____	$ _____

OVERTIME PERMIT

Employee: Date:

Department/Section: Time Clock No.:

    The above employee is authorized to work overtime a maximum of   hours
between   and   ,
for the purpose of:

    The overtime rate shall be according to company policy.

Comments/Conditions

_____

_____

_____

_____

_____

_____

_____

_____

_____

Requested by: _____

Approved by: _____

OVERTIME REPORT

Department: _____ Date: _____

Payroll Period   Total Hours   Total Salaries   Percent of Payroll

_____   _____

Approval Requested By   Date

_____   _____

Approved By   Date

PAST-DUE ACCOUNT

ACCOUNT NAME _____   TELEPHONE _____

ADDRESS _____

_____

EMPLOYER _____   TELEPHONE _____

ADDRESS _____

_____

GUARANTOR _____   TELEPHONE _____

ADDRESS _____

_____

DATE ACCOUNT OPENED _____   ORIGINAL BALANCE DUE _____

DATE DELINQUENT FILE _____

PAYMENT DATE	AMOUNT PAID	BALANCE DUE	PAYMENT DATE	AMOUNT PAID	BALANCE DUE

DATE	COLLECTION EFFORTS

135

PAYROLL REGISTER

I.D. #	Employee Name	Year-To-Date Total Earnings	Income Tax	Total Hours Worked	Base Pay	Earnings Regular	OT	Other	Total	Deductions Fed Inc.Tax	Provincial Inc.Tax	CCP & EI	Net Pay

PERSONAL GUARANTOR INFORMATION

Name:_____ Date: _____

Address:_____ Phone: _____

City: _____ Province:_____ Postal Code: _____

Affiliation with customer: _____ _____

Employed by:_____ _____

Address:_____ Phone: _____

Position:_____ _____

Annual salary: $ _____Employed since:_____

Other income: _____

_____

Credit References: (name and address)

_____

_____

_____

Bank Name: _____

Bank Account Number: _____

Credit Cards:

Am.Ex _____ M/C _____

Visa _____ _____

If you are a defendant in a lawsuit, please describe: _____

_____

Judgments:_____ _____

Bankruptcy within past 10 years:_____

Other outstanding obligations:_____

_____

    I certify the information in this application is true and may be relied upon for purposes of granting credit.

_____

PERSONNEL ACTIVITY REPORT

Period from:_____ to _____

Date prepared: _____ Prepared by:_____

	SALARIED	HOURLY	PART-TIME
# employees at start of period			
# employees at end of period			
# positions presently open			
# applicants interviewed			
# applicants hired			
% applicants hired during period			
# employees terminated			
# employees resigned			
# openings at start of period			
# openings at end of period			
Total requisitions to be filled			
Requisitions received			
Requisitions filled			
Requisitions unfilled			
Turnover rate for period			
Other:			

Notes: _____

_____

_____

_____

_____

138

PETTY CASH JOURNAL

OPENING BALANCE $_____

Date	Purpose	Amount	Spent By	Account	Balance
TOTAL					

Summary	
Account	Amount

Beginning Balance   _____

Less: Total Amount Spent   — _____

Expected Cash on Hand   = _____

Actual Cash on Hand   — _____

Shortage/(Overage)   = _____

Balanced By: _____

Date: _____

Approved By: _____

PHYSICIAN'S REPORT

Doctor _____ Date _____

Address _____

RE: _____

Dear Doctor:

Company policy requires that we verify extended medical absence. The above named employee, under your care, has been absent on the following dates: _____.

Please complete below and return for our records.

Very truly yours,

_____

Physician's Report

I certify that _____ has been under my medical care and that the absences on the dates listed were medically necessary or reasonable based on Mr./Ms. _____ medical condition.

Dated: _____   _____

Physician's Signature

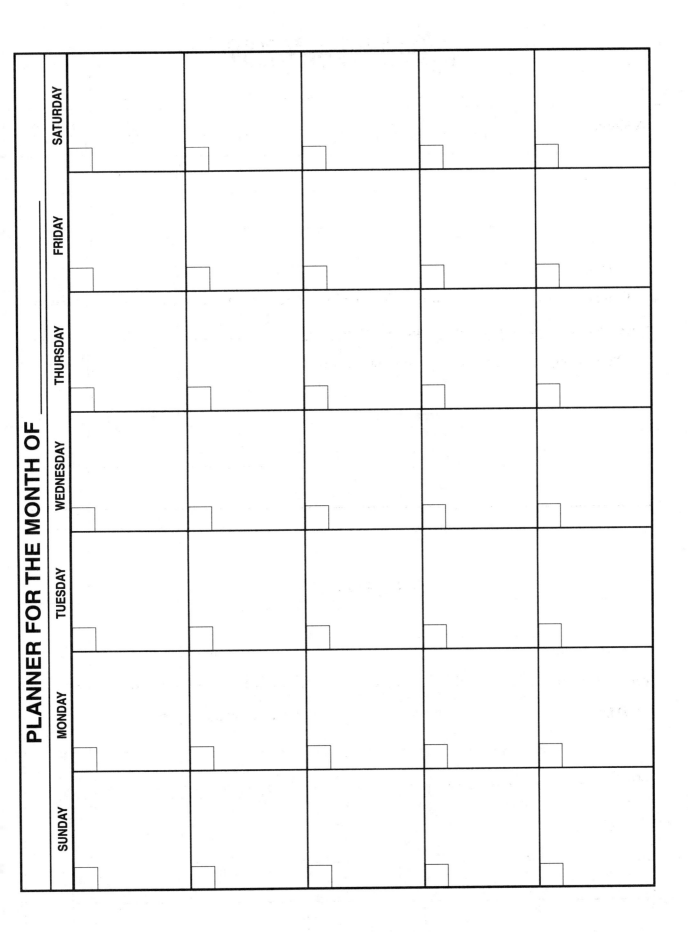

PLANNER FOR THE MONTH OF _____

SUNDAY	MONDAY	TUESDAY	WEDNESDAY	THURSDAY	FRIDAY	SATURDAY

PRIORITIES FOR TODAY

DATE:

ACTIVITY BY PRIORITY	COMPLETED ✓	FOLLOW-UP
1.		
2.		
3.		
4.		
5.		
6.		
7.		
8.		
9.		
10.		
11.		
12.		
13.		
14.		
15.		
16.		
17.		
18.		
19.		
20.		

PRODUCT INFORMATION SHEET

Product _____

Brand Name _____

I.D.# _____

Product Description _____

_____

_____

Features _____

_____

_____

_____

_____

Applications _____

_____

_____

_____

_____

Technical Specifications _____

_____

_____

_____

_____

Materials Required _____

_____

_____

_____

_____

Distributors _____

_____

_____

_____

Required Lead Time _____

Prepared by _____ Date _____

Approved by _____ Date _____

PRODUCT / INVENTORY PLANNER

PRODUCT	DESCRIPTION	SALES PRICE	COST	INVENTORY ON ORDER	INVENTORY ON HAND	INVENTORY TO SHIP	ORDER LEAD TIME

PRODUCT ITEMIZATION COST WORKSHEET

Product:	Quantity:		Date:	
Item	Description		Cost per Unit	Total Cost
Unit 1			$	$
Materials				
Set-up Charge				
Tool Cost				
Freight In				
Labor				
Unit 2				
Materials				
Set-up Charge				
Tool Cost				
Freight In				
Labor				
Unit 3				
Materials				
Set-up Charge				
Tool Cost				
Freight In				
Labor				
Unit 4				
Materials				
Set-up Charge				
Tool Cost				
Freight In				
Labor				
Unit 5				
Materials				
Set-up Charge				
Tool Cost				
Freight In				
Labor				
Product Packaging				
Set-up Charges				
Tooling Costs				
Freight In				
Labor				
Assembly Labor				
Finishing Labor				
Royalty				
Overhead				
Other				
Other				
TOTALS			$	$

PRODUCTION ANALYSIS

DATE: _____ DATES COVERED: _____

PRODUCT IDENTIFICATION	TOTAL NO. OF ORDERS	PENDING ORDERS	% TOTAL PRODUCTION	RETURNS	RETURN REASON

PRODUCTION ORDER

CUSTOMER: ORDER NO.:

Product Description	Cost	Price	Qty. On Hand

Required Materials	Product No.	Cost	On Hand	Out of Stock	Lead Time

DATE (ESTIMATED) OF COMPLETION:

PROFESSIONAL BILLING LOG

Date/Time	Client	Time	
		Hrs.	Min.

PROFITABILITY ANALYSIS

	SALES					PROFITS			
	Projection		Actual			Projection		Actual	
	Month	YTD	Month	YTD		Month	YTD	Month	YTD
JANUARY									
FEBRUARY									
MARCH									
APRIL									
MAY									
JUNE									
JULY									
AUGUST									
SEPTEMBER									
OCTOBER									
NOVEMBER									
DECEMBER									

COSTS

	Projection		Actual	
	Month	YTD	Month	YTD

Prepared By: _____

Date: _____

149

PRO-FORMA INCOME STATEMENTS

ITEM	PERIODS			
REVENUES				
Less: Returns & Allowances				
Net Revenues				
COST OF GOODS SOLD				
Net Margin				
EXPENSES				
Selling				
Salaries				
Advertising				
Other				
General/Administrative				
Salaries				
Employee Benefits				
Professional Services				
Rents				
Insurance				
Depreciation				
Amortization				
Office Supplies				
Interest				
Utilities				
Bad Debts/Doubtful Accounts				
Other				
Total Expenses				
Net Income Before Taxes				
Provision For Taxes				
Net Income After Taxes				
Prior Period Adjustment				
Net Increase (Decrease) to Retained Earnings				

PROGRAM PASSWORDS AND CODES

Program:	Password:	PIN:

PROJECT ACTIVITY PLANNER

PROJECT	ACTIVITY	TIME REQUIRED	✓	FOLLOW-UP

COMMENTS

PROJECT ASSIGNMENTS

DATE ASSIGNED	PROJECT	PERSON ASSIGNED TO	DUE DATE	COMMENTS

PROJECT CONTROL LOG

Name of Project	Description	Person Responsible	Date Assigned	Date Completed	Date of Last Review

PROJECT CONTROL SCHEDULE

Project	Assigned To	Scheduled Completion Date	Prior Review Date

PROJECT EXPENSES

NAME OF PROJECT:

SUMMARY NO.:

WEEK ENDING:

JOB	ORIGINAL REVISED JOB COMPLETION COST	ACTUAL COST (CURRENT)	% COMPLETED	PRESENT VALUE	OVERRUN/(UNDERRUN)			PREVIOUS REVISED JOB COMPLETION COST	CURRENT REVISED JOB COMPLETION COST
					THIS WEEK'S	LAST WEEK'S	DIFFER-ENCE		
TOTALS									

PROJECT PLAN

SCHEDULED		ACTUAL		PROJECT	✓
START	COMPLETE	START	COMPLETE		

PROJECT RECAP

Project title/no.:

Date started:

Planned completion date:

Estimated project cost:

Cost to complete:

REVIEW

(year-to-date)

Budget: Employee hours _____ $ _____ $_____ (as of)

Actual: Employee hours_____ $ _____ $_____ _____

Progress to date:

Comments:

By: _____ Review date: _____

PROJECT REVIEW

PROJECT MANAGER	NATURE OF PROJECT	DATE ASSIGNED	COMPLETION DATES			
			PRELIMINARY DUE DATE	REVIEWED BY	FINAL DUE DATE	REVIEWED BY

PROJECT SCHEDULE

PROJECT	ASSIGNED TO	DATE STARTED	SCHEDULED COMPLETION DATE	PRESENT PROGRESS

PURCHASE ORDER

DATE:

VENDOR: **SHIP TO:**

SHIP VIA	F.O.B. POINT	TERMS	DATE REQUIRED	P.O. NO.

QUANTITY		DESCRIPTION OF ITEM	PRICE	UNIT	AMOUNT
ORDERED	RECEIVED				

IMPORTANT
This Purchase Order Number must appear
on all invoices, acknowledgments, bills of
lading, correspondence and shipping cartons.

AUTHORIZED SIGNATURE _____

161

PURCHASE ORDER

P.O. NO.	
DATE	
DATE REQUIRED	
TERMS	
SHIP VIA	
F.O.B. POINT	

VENDOR

_____

_____

_____

SHIP TO

_____

_____

_____

QTY.	UNIT	ITEM	UNIT PRICE	AMOUNT

IMPORTANT
This Purchase Order Number must appear on all invoices, acknowledgments, bills of lading, correspondence and shipping cartons.

Please notify us immediately if you cannot ship complete order by date specified. STATE RESALE NUMBER:

_____

❏ RESALE   ❏ USE

AUTHORIZED SIGNATURE

PURCHASE ORDER LOG
From _____ **To** _____

Date Ordered	P.O. Number	Description	Date Shipped	Date Received	Invoice Number	Amount

TOTAL_____

PURCHASE ORDER REQUEST

Date _____   Request No. _____

I request that the following items be purchased.

Department _____   Notify _____

Intended Use _____   Charge To _____

Source _____   Ship Via _____

Comments _____

Quantity	Unit	Stock Number	Description	Date Needed	Estimated Cost

Requested By _____   For Purchasing Department Use:

Supervisor Approval _____   Authorized Approval _____

Ordered From _____   P.O. No. _____ Date _____

PURCHASE ORDER REQUISITION

DATE _____   REQUISITION NO. _____

PLEASE PURCHASE THE FOLLOWING

FOR DEPT. _____   PERSON TO BE NOTIFIED _____

VENDOR _____   CHARGE TO _____

NOTES _____   SHIP VIA _____

QUANTITY	UNIT	STOCK NO.	DESCRIPTION	DATE NEEDED	EST. COST

REQUESTED BY _____   FOR PURCHASING DEPT. USE ONLY:

DEPT. AUTHORIZATION _____   APPROVED _____

ORDERED FROM _____

P.O. NO. _____ DATE _____

PURCHASE REQUISITION

☐ CONFIRM ORDER

PURCHASED FROM _____ PURCHASE ORDER NO. _____

_____ DATE_____

FOR DEPT._____ DATE WANTED_____

F.O.B. POINT _____ TERMS_____ SHIP VIA_____

QUANTITY	DESCRIPTION	PRICE	UNIT

AUTHORIZED SIGNATURE _____

PURCHASE REQUISITION LOG

Requisition No.	Date Received	Item	Symbol	Quantity	Buyer's Name	Bids Req.	P.O. No.	Order Date	Name of Vendor	Invoice Received	Invoice Passed

QUALITY CONTROL RECORD

Page #:_____

Product:_____

Qty. per Sample: _____

Samples: _____

Remarks: _____

Employee: _____ From_____To _____

Employee: _____ From_____To _____

Employee: _____ From_____To _____

DATE	TIME	SAMPLE NUMBER	NO. DEFECTS	+ ✓	− ✓	DATE	TIME	SAMPLE NUMBER	NO. DEFECTS	+ ✓	− ✓

QUARTERLY EXPENSE SUMMARY

FOR YEAR ENDING: _____

MONTH	PHONE/FAX	TRAVEL	HOTEL	MEALS	ENTERTAINMENT	OTHER	MONTHLY TOTAL
JANUARY							
FEBRUARY							
MARCH							
1st QTR. TOTAL							
3-month TOTAL							
APRIL							
MAY							
JUNE							
2nd QTR.TOTAL							
6-month TOTAL							
JULY							
AUGUST							
SEPTEMBER							
3rd QTR.TOTAL							
9-month TOTAL							
OCTOBER							
NOVEMBER							
DECEMBER							
4th QTR. TOTAL							
YEARLY TOTAL							

REMARKS:

QUARTERLY SALES RECORD

Month _____
Daily Receipts

Day	Amount
1	_____
2	_____
3	_____
4	_____
5	_____
6	_____
7	_____
8	_____
9	_____
10	_____
11	_____
12	_____
13	_____
14	_____
15	_____
16	_____
17	_____
18	_____
19	_____
20	_____
21	_____
22	_____
23	_____
24	_____
25	_____
26	_____
27	_____
28	_____
29	_____
30	_____
31	_____

Total For Month _____

Total For Year To Date _____

Comments:

Prepared by: _____

Month _____
Daily Receipts

Day	Amount
1	_____
2	_____
3	_____
4	_____
5	_____
6	_____
7	_____
8	_____
9	_____
10	_____
11	_____
12	_____
13	_____
14	_____
15	_____
16	_____
17	_____
18	_____
19	_____
20	_____
21	_____
22	_____
23	_____
24	_____
25	_____
26	_____
27	_____
28	_____
29	_____
30	_____
31	_____

Total For Month _____

Total For Year To Date _____

Comments:

Prepared by: _____

Month _____
Daily Receipts

Day	Amount
1	_____
2	_____
3	_____
4	_____
5	_____
6	_____
7	_____
8	_____
9	_____
10	_____
11	_____
12	_____
13	_____
14	_____
15	_____
16	_____
17	_____
18	_____
19	_____
20	_____
21	_____
22	_____
23	_____
24	_____
25	_____
26	_____
27	_____
28	_____
29	_____
30	_____
31	_____

Total For Month _____

Total For Year To Date _____

Comments:

Prepared by: _____

QUOTATION

DATE

F.O.B.

TO

TERMS

DELIVERY

THANK YOU FOR YOUR INQUIRY OF _____ NO.: _____

WE ARE PLEASED TO PROVIDE THE FOLLOWING QUOTE:

QUANTITY	ITEM	PRICE

WE SHALL SUPPLY ANY FURTHER INFORMATION YOU REQUEST.

PER _____

QUOTATION RECORD

ITEM _____

DESCRIPTION _____

_____

DATE REQUIRED _____

SPECIFICATION NO. _____

UNIT _____

PURCHASE DATE	QUANTITY ORDER NO.	LIST PURCHASED	PRICE	NET DISCOUNT	PRICE	TOTAL FREIGHT	UNIT COST	COST	VENDOR	REMARKS

RECEIPT FOR COMPANY PROPERTY

Employee

ID No.

Department/Section

    I acknowledge receiving the company equipment listed. I shall maintain the equipment in good condition and shall return it when I stop working for the company, or earlier upon request. I will report any loss or damage immediately. I will use the property for work-related purposes only.

Received			Returned	
Item	Quantity	No. or I.D.	Returned To (Initial)	Date Returned
_____	_____	_____	_____	_____
_____	_____	_____	_____	_____
_____	_____	_____	_____	_____
_____	_____	_____	_____	_____
_____	_____	_____	_____	_____
_____	_____	_____	_____	_____
_____	_____	_____	_____	_____
_____	_____	_____	_____	_____
_____	_____	_____	_____	_____
_____	_____	_____	_____	_____

_____

Employee Signature

_____

Department

_____

Date

RECEIVING RECORD

From _____ To _____

DATE ORDERED	P.O. NUMBER	ISSUED TO	DESCRIPTION	DATE RECEIVED	INVOICE NUMBER	FREIGHT BILL NUMBER	HOW PAID	RECEIVED BY

RECORD ACCOUNT

SECTION:

TITLE	CHARACTERISTICS	SOURCE	SIZE	DATA	AMOUNT	FREQUENCY

RECORD OF INTERNET PURCHASES

Date of Order	Product No. / Description of Item (quantity, color, etc.)	Website / URL	Company Address	Phone	Sale Price	Amt. Paid	Check #	Credit Card	Money Order	C.O.D.	Received	Follow-up Info: (date contacted contact person action taken)

RECORD OF PURCHASES BY MAIL ORDER

Date of Order	Product No. / Description of Item (quantity, color, etc.)	Ordered From	Company Address	Company Phone	Sale Price	Amt. Paid	Check #	Credit Card	Money Order	C.O.D.	Received	Follow-up Info: (date contacted contact person action taken)

RECORD OF SUBSCRIPTIONS

Publication	Date Ordered	Cost	Check # / Credit Card	Term	First Issue Received	Monthly Receipt Date	Month of Expiration	How Acquired	Agent	Address	Gift To	Personal

RECORD OF TAX DEDUCTIBLE CONTRIBUTIONS

Date	Donation to	Amount or Value	Cash	Check	Check #	Receipt

RECORD OF TAX DEDUCTIBLE EXPENSES

Date	Description / To Whom	Check Number	Amount or Value of Deduction		
			Tax/Int	Medical	Other (list)

REQUEST FOR QUOTE

DATE: POINT OF DELIVERY:

PLEASE QUOTE BEST PRICE AND DELIVERY ON THE BELOW ITEMS.

ALL PRICES QUOTED F.O.B.	TERMS	SHIP VIA	EARLIEST SHIPPING DATE	
QUANTITY	DESCRIPTION		PRICE	AMOUNT

THIS IS NOT AN ORDER   BY _____

REQUEST FOR QUOTE

Quote Requested From:

_____
Sub-contractor/Contractor

Respond By:

_____

Blue Prints Available For Review ❑ Yes ❑ No

THIS IS NOT AN ORDER

DATE
_____

JOB SITE ADDRESS
_____
_____

PLEASE QUOTE THE FOLLOWING WORK FOR _____
General Contractor

AT _____
General Contractor's Address

PRICES QUOTED F.O.B.	TERMS	WORK TO START ON OR BEFORE	EARLIEST DATE AVAILABLE FOR WORK

DESCRIPTION OF WORK		LABOR	MATERIAL

By _____

182

REQUEST FOR SAMPLE

Date _____

Ship To:

Name _____ Title _____ Tel/Ext _____

Company _____

Address _____

City/Province/Postal Code _____

❏ New Customer   ❏ Existing Customer   ❏ Charge   ❏ No Charge

Quantity	Item Description	Total

Ship Via: _____

Signed: _____ Authorized By: _____

REQUEST FOR TRANSFER

Employee Name		Payroll No.	Shift
Department			
Present Position		Hire Date	
Position Requested			
Reason For Transfer			
Employee's Signature		Date	Tel/Ext

SUPERVISOR'S COMMENTS

Evaluation In Present Job

Comments

Action Taken

Supervisor's Signature		Date	Tel/Ext

184

ROUTING INSTRUCTIONS

DATE
ATTENTION
RE:

TO

PLEASE

- ❑ REVIEW AND FILE
- ❑ REVIEW AND RETURN
- ❑ REVIEW AND RETURN WITH COMMENTS
- ❑ FOR YOUR APPROVAL
- ❑ FOR YOUR USE
- ❑ FOR YOUR SIGNATURE
- ❑ PREPARE FOR MY SIGNATURE
- ❑ PREPARE FOR _____ SIGNATURE

- ❑ INVESTIGATE AND REPORT TO ME
- ❑ INVESTIGATE AND REPORT TO _____
- ❑ RESUBMIT WITH _____ COPIES
- ❑ ATTACHED IS: ❑ APPROVED   ❑ REJECTED
- ❑ MAKE NOTED CHANGES
- ❑ _____

- ❑ SEE ME ABOUT   ❑ ATTACHED   ❑ ABOVE ON
_____ AT _____AM/PM

NOTES

BY	PREPARED FOR/APPROVED BY	
TITLE	TITLE	
LOCATION	LOCATION	
PHONE	DATE	PHONE	DATE

SALARY CHANGE NOTICE

Employee No.	Name		Effective Date

Job Title

Department

Social Insurance No.	Employment Date

Time in Present Job

Attendance in Past 12 Months

	Paid Absences	Non-Paid Absences	Late	

Use Figures To Match Range

Range _____ To _____ Present Salary _____

Recommended Increase _____ Recommended New Salary _____

Status After Increase

❑ Exempt   ❑ Non-exempt

Reason For Changes

❑ Hired	❑ Promotion	❑ Layoff
❑ Re-hired	❑ Demotion	❑ Resignation
❑ Temporary Employment Extended	❑ Transfer	❑ Retirement
❑ Completed Probation	❑ Merit Increase	❑ Dismissal
❑ Reevaluation	❑ Union Scale	❑ Other
❑ Leave of Absence		
❑ Maternity	❑ Schooling	❑ Military
❑ Medical	❑ Personal	❑ Other

Comments:

_____

_____

_____

_____

Approved by _____   Date _____

❑ S/M ❑ Hourly	For Sal. Admin. and Payroll Use			Non-exempt
Present Rate Annual	New Rate Annual	S/M Increase	Annual Increase	Hrly. Rate

SALES ACTIVITY ANALYSIS BY MONTH

NAME OF SALESPERSON: TERRITORY: PREPARED BY:

		JAN	FEB	MAR	APR	MAY	JUN	JUL	AUG	SEP	OCT	NOV	DEC	YEARLY TOTAL
PROFIT	Gross Sales													
	Gross Profit													
	% Gross Profit to Gross Sales													
	Net Profit													
	% Net Profit to Gross Sales													
SALES COST	Salary													
	Commission													
	Expense: Auto													
	Travel													
	Telephone/Fax													
	Entertainment													
	Misc.													
ACCT. INFO	Total Days Worked													
	No. Calls Made													
	Avg. Calls Per Day													
ACTIVITY	No. Accts. Activated													
	No. Accts. Deactivated													
	No. Accts. at Month End													
	No. Potential Accts.													

SALES CALL LOG

Number _____ Date _____

Name of Company _____

Contact _____ Phone _____

Type of Call: ❑ Customer   ❑ Prospect

Comments _____
_____
_____

Purpose of Call _____
_____

Opening Conversation _____
_____
_____
_____

Sales Story _____
_____
_____
_____

Benefits to Customer _____
_____
_____
_____

Objections or Resistance Response _____
_____
_____
_____

Closing Conversation _____
_____
_____
_____

When to Follow Up _____
_____

SALES LEAD

SALES APPOINTMENT   SOURCE

DATE:

DAY:

TIME:

NAME OF CONTACT:

ADDRESS:

PHONE/FAX:

E-MAIL:

EXPRESSED INTEREST IN:

NOTES:

SALES PROJECTIONS BY MONTH

	NEW BUSINESS			REORDERS			TOTAL		
SALESPERSON / DEPARTMENT					DATE				
	EST.	ACTUAL	+ / −	EST.	ACTUAL	+ / −	EST.	ACTUAL	+ / −
JAN									
FEB									
MAR									
APR									
MAY									
JUN									
JUL									
AUG									
SEP									
OCT									
NOV									
DEC									
YEAR									

PREPARED BY:

SALES PROSPECT FILE

New ❑   Update ❑   Follow-up date:

Company:

Contact: Title:

Address:

Beset time to contact:

Telephone: Fax: E-mail:

Market segment:

Call-in ❑   Referral ❑

Current supplier:

Approximate monthly volume:

Form letters sent:

Literature sent:

Samples sent:

Sales calls (date and summary):

Date and summary of last contact:

Desirability as client: Very high ❑   High ❑   Medium ❑   Low ❑

Possibility of closing: 100% ❑   90% ❑   70% ❑   50% ❑   30% ❑   None ❑

Remarks:

SALES RECORD

Name: _____

Name of Account	Account #	Date of Sale	Amount of Sale
_____	_____	_____	$ _____
_____	_____	_____	$ _____
_____	_____	_____	$ _____
_____	_____	_____	$ _____
_____	_____	_____	$ _____
_____	_____	_____	$ _____
_____	_____	_____	$ _____
_____	_____	_____	$ _____
_____	_____	_____	$ _____
_____	_____	_____	$ _____
_____	_____	_____	$ _____
_____	_____	_____	$ _____
_____	_____	_____	$ _____
_____	_____	_____	$ _____
_____	_____	_____	$ _____
_____	_____	_____	$ _____
_____	_____	_____	$ _____
_____	_____	_____	$ _____
_____	_____	_____	$ _____
_____	_____	_____	$ _____
_____	_____	_____	$ _____

Total Sales: $ _____

SEPARATION REPORT

Company   Date

Employee

Social Insurance No.   Job/Title

Name of Supervisor

1. Termination Date   Pay Thru

2. Cause of Termination

3. Unemployment Compensation Eligibility

4. Benefits Eligibility

5. Overall Assessment of Employee

6. Employee Eligibility for Rehire?

7. Comments:

_____
                                    Supervisor

ATTACH SUPPORTING DOCUMENTS AS APPLICABLE
USE REVERSE IF YOU NEED ADDITIONAL SPACE

SEVEN-DAY APPOINTMENT SCHEDULE

	SUNDAY	MONDAY	TUESDAY	WEDNESDAY	THURSDAY	FRIDAY	SATURDAY	
8:00								8:00
9:00								9:00
10:00								10:00
11:00								11:00
12:00								12:00
1:00								1:00
2:00								2:00
3:00								3:00
4:00								4:00
5:00								5:00
6:00								6:00
7:00								7:00
8:00								8:00
9:00								9:00
10:00								10:00
11:00								11:00
12:00								12:00

REMARKS:

SEVEN-DAY APPOINTMENT SCHEDULE

	SUNDAY	MONDAY	TUESDAY	WEDNESDAY	THURSDAY	FRIDAY	SATURDAY	
8:00								8:00
8:30								8:30
9:00								9:00
9:30								9:30
10:00								10:00
10:30								10:30
11:00								11:00
11:30								11:30
12:00								12:00
12:30								12:30
1:00								1:00
1:30								1:30
2:00								2:00
2:30								2:30
3:00								3:00
3:30								3:30
4:00								4:00
4:30								4:30
5:00								5:00
5:30								5:30

SHIPPING ORDER

SHIP TO:

DATE:

CUST. ORDER NO.:

INVOICE NO.:

QUANTITY ORDERED	QUANTITY SHIPPED	ITEMS

Received by_____ Per _____ Date _____

SHORT PAY INQUIRY

Date:

To:

Thank you for your payment for our invoice number _____ . However, we were unable to determine why there was a short pay on the order. Please tell us why you are not paying the full amount.

Sincerely,

_____

Amount short-paid $ _____   Reference # _____

_____

From:_____

Reason:_____

_____

_____

_____

SIGHT DRAFT

Date:

To: _____
     (Bank)

Upon presentment, you are directed to pay to the order of
the sum of   Dollars ($) and debit my
account for said amount.

_____
Account Name

By: _____
     Authorized Signatory

_____
Account Number

SOFTWARE INVENTORY

Software			Release Date	Date Received
Modification	Date Rec'd.	Date Updated	Notes	

SOFTWARE INVENTORY

Title: Format: Date Purchased: Comments:

_____   _____   _____   _____
_____   _____   _____   _____
_____   _____   _____   _____
_____   _____   _____   _____
_____   _____   _____   _____
_____   _____   _____   _____
_____   _____   _____   _____
_____   _____   _____   _____
_____   _____   _____   _____
_____   _____   _____   _____
_____   _____   _____   _____
_____   _____   _____   _____
_____   _____   _____   _____
_____   _____   _____   _____
_____   _____   _____   _____
_____   _____   _____   _____
_____   _____   _____   _____
_____   _____   _____   _____
_____   _____   _____   _____
_____   _____   _____   _____
_____   _____   _____   _____
_____   _____   _____   _____
_____   _____   _____   _____
_____   _____   _____   _____

STAFF REQUISITION

Department: _____ Date: _____

Job Title: _____

Refer Applicant To: _____ Telephone Number & Ext.: _____

Requested Starting Date: _____ Hours: _____

Job Description: _____

_____

_____

Job Requirements: _____

_____

_____

Applicant's Experience: _____

_____

Will Consider: ❑ Transfer Applicants ❑ Outside Applicants

Replacement: ❑ Yes ❑ No

          Name of Employee Being Replaced: _____

          End Date: _____

          Final Salary: _____

Increase Staff: ❑ Yes ❑ No

If yes, state why additional employee is needed: _____

_____

_____

_____

QUALIFICATIONS

College/Univ. Graduate: ❑ Yes ❑ No Typing (wpm): _____

Professional Degrees (specify): _____ Shorthand (wpm): _____

Computer Experience: ❑ Yes ❑ No Applications _____

Other Qualifications: _____

_____

_____

_____

Job Responsibilities and Expectations: _____

_____

_____

_____

Approvals must be obtained prior to submission to Human Resources

Submitted by: _____

Approved by: _____

FOR HUMAN RESOURCES USE ONLY

Date Received _____ Date Filled _____ By _____

202

STATEMENT OF
ACCRUED BENEFITS

Employee _____ Department _____

Total Value of Benefits Accrued To Date _____

Severance Pay $_____

Accrued Reimbursable Expenses $_____

Credit Union Balance $_____

Cash Value Life Insurance $_____

Company Shares Held   _____

Stock Dividend Value $_____

Vested Pension $_____

Non-Vested Pension $_____

Profit Sharing - Vested $_____

Profit Sharing - Non-Vested $_____

Accrued Sick Days   _____

Accrued Sick Pay $_____

Accrued Vacation Days   _____

Accrued Vacation Pay $_____

Other Benefits:

_____   _____

_____   _____

_____   _____

_____   _____

This is an ❏ Interim ❏ Final Statement.

This statement is subject to corrections.

_____   _____
Signed   Date

STATEMENT

DATE

INVOICE NO.

TERMS

AMT. PAID

PLEASE DETACH AND RETURN WITH YOUR REMITTANCE

DATE	INVOICE NO./DESCRIPTION	CHARGE	CREDIT	BALANCE

PLEASE PAY THIS AMOUNT ➡

SUPERVISOR'S / NEW HIRE CHECKLIST

Employee Name _____ Department _____ Ext _____

Hire Date _____ Title / Position _____

The following have been reviewed with _____
Name of Employee

Departmental Functions and Goals   _____

Work Schedule   _____

Co-worker Introductions   _____

Locker / Desk / Office   _____

Supplies & Storage / Requisitions   _____

Company Safety Procedures   _____

Personnel Office / Benefits Coordinator / HR Officer _____

Overtime Policy   _____

Notice Postings   _____

Other:

_____   _____

_____   _____

_____   _____

_____   _____

Date _____

I have received the above checked information and I acknowledge that I understand it.

_____   _____
Employee   Supervisor

TELEMARKETING CALLBACK

DATE OF CALL:

TELEMARKETING REPRESENTATIVE:

NUMBER OF THIS CALL:

ACCOUNT/ PROSPECT:

MAILING ADDRESS:

DELIVERY ADDRESS:

SPECIAL INSTRUCTIONS:

BUSINESS TELEPHONE:

FAX: E-MAIL:

CONTACT:

PREFERRED METHOD:

TIME:

PLACE:

OBJECTIVE(S) OF THIS CALL:

OBJECTIVE(S) OF LAST CALL:

LAST PURCHASE DATE AND ITEM/SERVICE:

CURRENT SALES POTENTIAL:

FUTURE SALES POTENTIAL:

REFERRAL POTENTIAL:

REMARKS:

NEXT FOLLOW-UP DATE:

TELEMARKETING CONTROL

DATE:

NAME OF PROSPECT:

ADDRESS:

BUSINESS TELEPHONE:

FAX:

E-MAIL:

DELIVERY INSTRUCTIONS:

PREFERRED CONTACT:

METHOD:

TIME:

PLACE:

REASON FOR CALL:

PREVIOUS PURCHASE (IF ANY):

CURRENT SALE:

FUTURE POTENTIAL:

POTENTIAL REFERENCE:

REMARKS:

FOLLOW-UP:

CALLER'S SIGNATURE: _____

TELEPHONE/FAX INDEX

Name and Address	Telephone Number	Fax Number

TELEPHONE LOG

PERSON CALLED	COMPANY	TELEPHONE NO.	REASON	COM-PLETED RETURN ✓	CALL BACK ✓	WILL ✓	NOTES

209

TELEPHONE REFERENCE RECORD

Reference Given on Employee _____

Date & Person Inquiring _____ Time _____

Company _____

Address _____

_____ Phone No. _____

Reason For Inquiry _____

_____

_____

_____

_____

_____

Specific Questions/Replies _____

_____

_____

_____

_____

_____

_____

_____

_____

_____

_____
Submitted By

TEMPORARY EMPLOYMENT REQUEST

Date _____

Job Title _____

Description of Duties _____

Immediate Supervisor _____ Tel. _____ Ext. _____

Date Required : From _____ To _____

Shift Required: From _____ To _____

Reasons for Requisition _____

_____

_____

_____

_____

_____

_____

_____

_____

Estimated Cost _____

_____

Funds Available _____ ❑ Yes ❑ No

_____
Requested By

Date _____   _____
                                           Authorized By

30 MINUTE APPOINTMENT SCHEDULE

DAY:_____ DATE: _____

	APPOINTMENT	COMMENTS
7:00		
7:30		
8:00		
8:30		
9:00		
9:30		
10:00		
10:30		
11:00		
11:30		
12:00		
12:30		
1:00		
1:30		
2:00		
2:30		
3:00		
3:30		
4:00		
4:30		
5:00		
5:30		
6:00		
6:30		

30 MINUTE SCHEDULE

Time	
7:00	
7:30	
8:00	
8:30	
9:00	
9:30	
10:00	
10:30	
11:00	
11:30	
12:00	
12:30	
1:00	
1:30	
2:00	
2:30	
3:00	
3:30	
4:00	
4:30	
5:00	
5:30	

TIME AND MATERIAL REPORT

Job No. _____

Name _____ Date _____

Straight Time _____ Overtime _____

Total Hours _____   _____

WAGES _____   _____ TOTAL WAGES _____

Amount	Item	Unit Price	Total	COST SUMMARY
				Material
				Permit
				Labor
				Job Cost
				Profit
				Overhead
				Price of Job
				Gain
				Loss
				NOTES:

Comments:

TIME LOG

Name _____

Title _____

Department _____

Date _____

Time	Activity and Result	Total Time Spent
_____	_____	_____
_____	_____	_____
_____	_____	_____
_____	_____	_____
_____	_____	_____
_____	_____	_____
_____	_____	_____
_____	_____	_____
_____	_____	_____
_____	_____	_____
_____	_____	_____
_____	_____	_____
_____	_____	_____
_____	_____	_____
_____	_____	_____
_____	_____	_____
_____	_____	_____
_____	_____	_____
_____	_____	_____
_____	_____	_____
_____	_____	_____
_____	_____	_____
_____	_____	_____
_____	_____	_____
_____	_____	_____
_____	_____	_____
_____	_____	_____
_____	_____	_____

TIME PROJECTED/COMPLETED REVIEW

DATE:

PROJECTED		ACTUAL		ACTIVITY OR PROJECT	NOTES
TOTAL TIME	% OF TIME	TOTAL TIME	% OF TIME		

TOMORROW'S PRIORITIES

DATE:

| 1: URGENT | 2: IMPORTANT | 3: LOW PRIORITY | 4: DO (TIME PERMITTING) |

PRIORITY CODE		✓

TOP PRIORITY

DATE NEEDED	ITEM	✓

TRANSMITTAL LETTER

	DATE
	ATTENTION
TO	RE:

WE ARE SENDING ❑ ATTACHED ❑ UNDER SEPARATE COVER VIA _____

COPIES	DATE	NO.	DESCRIPTION

PURPOSE:

❑ FOR YOUR APPROVAL   ❑ APPROVED AS NOTED   ❑ RESUBMIT _____ COPIES FOR

❑ FOR YOUR USE   ❑ APPROVED AS SUBMITTED   APPROVAL

❑ FOR YOUR REVIEW   ❑ APPROVED AS CHANGED   ❑ SUBMIT _____ COPIES FOR

❑ FOR YOUR COMMENTS   ❑ REJECTED AS NOTED   DISTRIBUTION

❑ FOR YOUR SIGNATURE   ❑ REJECTED AS CHANGED   ❑ REVIEW _____ COPIES FOR

❑ FOR YOUR _____   ❑ RETURNED FOR CORRECTIONS   _____

❑ _____   ❑ _____

COMMENTS:

COPY TO	SIGNATURE	
	TITLE	DATE

URGENT MEMO

DATE:

TO: DEPARTMENT:

FROM: DEPARTMENT:

MESSAGE:

❑ FOR YOUR RECORDS
❑ ROUTE TO: _____
❑ REPLY REQUESTED IMMEDIATELY

DATE:

REPLY:

UTILITIES COST INVENTORY

Name: _____

Utility	Billing Date	Cost This Month	Cost Last Month
_____	_____	$_____	$_____
_____	_____	$_____	$_____
_____	_____	$_____	$_____
_____	_____	$_____	$_____
_____	_____	$_____	$_____
_____	_____	$_____	$_____
_____	_____	$_____	$_____
_____	_____	$_____	$_____
_____	_____	$_____	$_____
_____	_____	$_____	$_____
_____	_____	$_____	$_____
_____	_____	$_____	$_____
_____	_____	$_____	$_____
_____	_____	$_____	$_____
_____	_____	$_____	$_____
_____	_____	$_____	$_____
_____	_____	$_____	$_____
_____	_____	$_____	$_____
_____	_____	$_____	$_____
_____	_____	$_____	$_____
_____	_____	$_____	$_____
_____	_____	$_____	$_____
	Total:	$_____	$_____

VACATION REQUEST

EMPLOYEE: EMPLOYMENT DATE:

I REQUEST A   WEEK VACATION:

    FROM   THROUGH

MY ALTERNATE CHOICE IS:

    FROM   THROUGH

(IF A HOLIDAY OCCURS DURING YOUR VACATION, PLEASE REQUEST EXTRA DAYS BELOW

I PREFER TO SPLIT MY VACATION:

FIRST WEEK: FROM   THROUGH

SECOND WEEK: FROM   THROUGH

THIRD WEEK: FROM   THROUGH

FOURTH WEEK: FROM   THROUGH

BELOW VACATION DATES APPROVED BY:

DATE:

APPROVED VACATION DATES:

222

VACATION SCHEDULE

Today's Date _____

Name of Employee	Person to Cover Job	Month:	Month:	Month:	Month:	Month:	Other Weeks

223

VENDOR FILE

Name of Vendor _____ Contact _____

Address _____

Phone/Fax/E-mail _____

Vendor No. _____ Credit Rating _____

Delivery Time
   Freight _____ Express _____ Truck _____

Date	P.O. No.	Material	Symbol	Quantity	Comments

VENDOR PAYMENT REPORT

PERIOD: _____

FROM: _____   TO: _____

MONTH: _____

ACCOUNT D NUMBER	INVOICE	NAME OF VENDOR	ITEM DESCRIPTION	30 DAYS	60 DAYS	OVER 90 DAYS	TOTAL DUE
_____	_____	_____	_____	____	____	____	____
_____	_____	_____	_____	____	____	____	____
_____	_____	_____	_____	____	____	____	____
_____	_____	_____	_____	____	____	____	____
_____	_____	_____	_____	____	____	____	____
_____	_____	_____	_____	____	____	____	____
_____	_____	_____	_____	____	____	____	____
_____	_____	_____	_____	____	____	____	____
_____	_____	_____	_____	____	____	____	____
_____	_____	_____	_____	____	____	____	____
_____	_____	_____	_____	____	____	____	____
_____	_____	_____	_____	____	____	____	____
_____	_____	_____	_____	____	____	____	____
_____	_____	_____	_____	____	____	____	____
_____	_____	_____	_____	____	____	____	____
_____	_____	_____	_____	____	____	____	____
_____	_____	_____	_____	____	____	____	____
_____	_____	_____	_____	____	____	____	____
_____	_____	_____	_____	____	____	____	____
_____	_____	_____	_____	____	____	____	____
_____	_____	_____	_____	____	____	____	____
			TOTAL	____	____	____	____

VENDOR PRICE ANALYSIS

Name of Product and Product I.D. # _____

	Name of Vendor	Quantity						Other Factors		
		ea.	ea.	ea.	ea.	ea.	ea.	Lead Time	Est Del.	Terms / Conditions
1										
2										
3										
4										
5										
6										
7										
8										
9										
10										
11										
12										
13										
14										
15										
16										
17										

Department	Proposed By	Submitted To	Date

WEEKLY ACTIVITY REVIEW

WEEK OF:								FOLLOW-UP	✓
S	M	T	W	T	F	S			

WEEKLY APPOINTMENTS

WEEK OF:

	MONDAY	TUESDAY	WEDNESDAY	THURSDAY	FRIDAY
8:00					
8:30					
9:00					
9:30					
10:00					
10:30					
11:00					
11:30					
12:00					
12:30					
1:00					
1:30					
2:00					
2:30					
3:00					
3:30					
4:00					
4:30					
5:00					
5:30					

WEEKLY DEADLINES

Check Day Needed					Time Needed		Follow-Up	✔
M	T	W	T	F				

WEEK OF _____

WEEKLY PAYROLL RECAP

WEEK ENDING:

Employee	Hours Worked	Rate	TOTALS			DEDUCTIONS						Net Pay	Check
			Reg. Wages	O.T. Wages	Gross Wages	Federal Inc. Tax	Provincial Inc. Tax	CPP	EI	Dues	Other		

WEEKLY PAYROLL RECAP

Department	Supervisor	Location	Week Ending	Date

Name of Employee	Hours Reg./O.T.	Pay Rate	Payroll			Deductions						Net	Check #
			Reg. Wages	O.T. Wages	Gross Wages	Federal Inc. Tax	Provincial Inc. Tax	CPP	EI	Other	Other		

WEEKLY PETTY CASH RECORD

JOB/SHIFT: _____

DATE: _____   BEGINNING BALANCE: _____

SUPERVISOR: _____

DATE	PAID TO	PURPOSE	COST		BALANCE ON HAND

TOTAL _____

AMOUNT TO BE REIMBURSED $ _____

APPROVED BY: _____

WEEKLY TIME SHEETS

WEEK ENDING _____

Name of Employee	Mon	Tues	Wed	Thur	Fri	Sat	Sun	Total Hours	Gross Pay	Deduct	Net Pay
WEEKLY TOTALS											

WORK AUTHORIZATION

General Contractor		Date	Date To Be Completed
Address		Sub-contractor	
City/Province/Postal Code		Address	
Phone	Fax	City/Province/Postal Code	
E-mail		Phone	Fax
Job Site Name		E-mail	
Street Address			
City/Province/Postal Code			

DESCRIPTION OF WORK	AMOUNT	
	Labor Only	
	Materials	
	Sub-total	
	Tax	
	Total Amount	

Signature: _____

WORK OVERTIME REPORT

DATE:

Day	Started Work	Ended Work	Overtime	Notes

1	
2	
3	
4	
5	
6	
7	
8	
9	
10	
11	
12	
13	
14	
15	
16	
17	
18	
19	
20	
21	
22	
23	
24	
25	
26	
27	
28	
29	
30	
31	

1			
2			
3			
4			
5			
6			
7			
8			
9			
10			
11			
12			
13			
14			
15			
16			
17			
18			
19			
20			
21			
22			
23			
24			
25			
26			
27			
28			
29			
30			
31			

1				
2				
3				
4				
5				
6				
7				
8				
9				
10				
11				
12				
13				
14				
15				
16				
17				
18				
19				
20				
21				
22				
23				
24				
25				
26				
27				
28				
29				
30				
31				

1					
2					
3					
4					
5					
6					
7					
8					
9					
10					
11					
12					
13					
14					
15					
16					
17					
18					
19					
20					
21					
22					
23					
24					
25					
26					
27					
28					
29					
30					
31					

1						
2						
3						
4						
5						
6						
7						
8						
9						
10						
11						
12						
13						
14						
15						
16						
17						
18						
19						
20						
21						
22						
23						
24						
25						
26						
27						
28						
29						
30						
31						

1							
2							
3							
4							
5							
6							
7							
8							
9							
10							
11							
12							
13							
14							
15							
16							
17							
18							
19							
20							
21							
22							
23							
24							
25							
26							
27							
28							
29							
30							
31							

241

1							
2							
3							
4							
5							
6							
7							
8							
9							
10							
11							
12							
13							
14							
15							
16							
17							
18							
19							
20							
21							
22							
23							
24							
25							
26							
27							
28							
29							
30							
31							

1										
2										
3										
4										
5										
6										
7										
8										
9										
10										
11										
12										
13										
14										
15										
16										
17										
18										
19										
20										
21										
22										
23										
24										
25										
26										
27										
28										
29										
30										
31										

1									
2									
3									
4									
5									
6									
7									
8									
9									
10									
11									
12									
13									
14									
15									
16									
17									
18									
19									
20									
21									
22									
23									
24									
25									
26									
27									
28									
29									
30									
31									

1											
2											
3											
4											
5											
6											
7											
8											
9											
10											
11											
12											
13											
14											
15											
16											
17											
18											
19											
20											
21											
22											
23											
24											
25											
26											
27											
28											
29											
30											
31											

1										
2										
3										
4										
5										
6										
7										
8										
9										
10										
11										
12										
13										
14										
15										
16										
17										
18										
19										
20										
21										
22										
23										
24										
25										
26										
27										
28										
29										
30										
31										

1														
2														
3														
4														
5														
6														
7														
8														
9														
10														
11														
12														
13														
14														
15														
16														
17														
18														
19														
20														
21														
22														
23														
24														
25														
26														
27														
28														
29														
30														
31														

1															
2															
3															
4															
5															
6															
7															
8															
9															
10															
11															
12															
13															
14															
15															
16															
17															
18															
19															
20															
21															
22															
23															
24															
25															
26															
27															
28															
29															
30															
31															

1																		
2																		
3																		
4																		
5																		
6																		
7																		
8																		
9																		
10																		
11																		
12																		
13																		
14																		
15																		
16																		
17																		
18																		
19																		
20																		
21																		
22																		
23																		
24																		
25																		
26																		
27																		
28																		
29																		
30																		
31																		

	1
1	
2	
3	
4	
5	
6	
7	
8	
9	
10	
11	
12	
13	
14	
15	
16	
17	
18	
19	
20	
21	
22	
23	
24	
25	
26	
27	
28	
29	
30	
31	

1																		
2																		
3																		
4																		
5																		
6																		
7																		
8																		
9																		
10																		
11																		
12																		
13																		
14																		
15																		
16																		
17																		
18																		
19																		
20																		
21																		
22																		
23																		
24																		
25																		
26																		
27																		
28																		
29																		
30																		
31																		

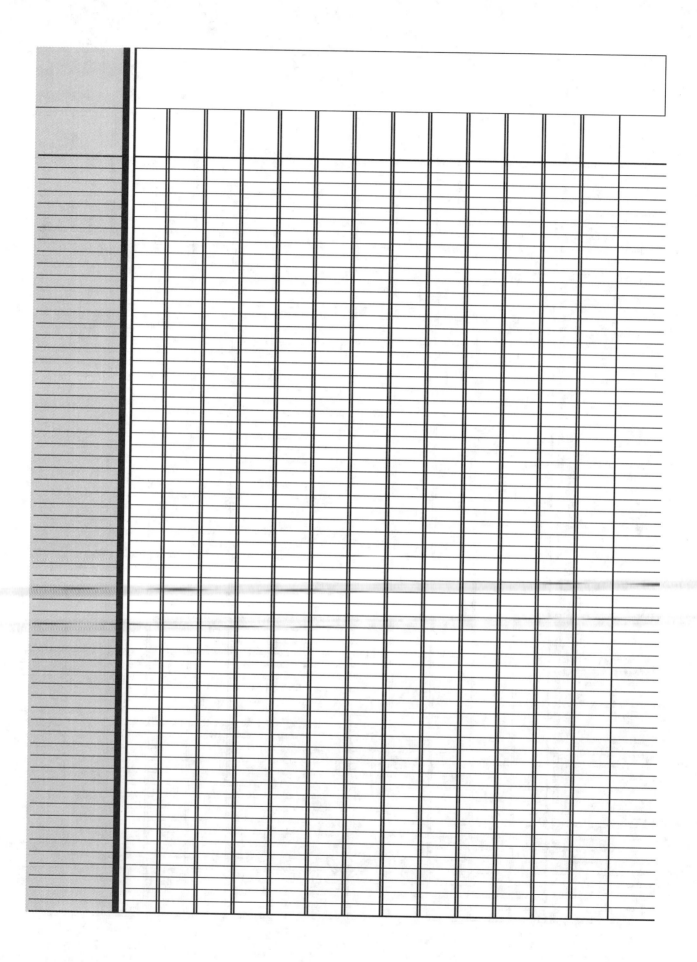

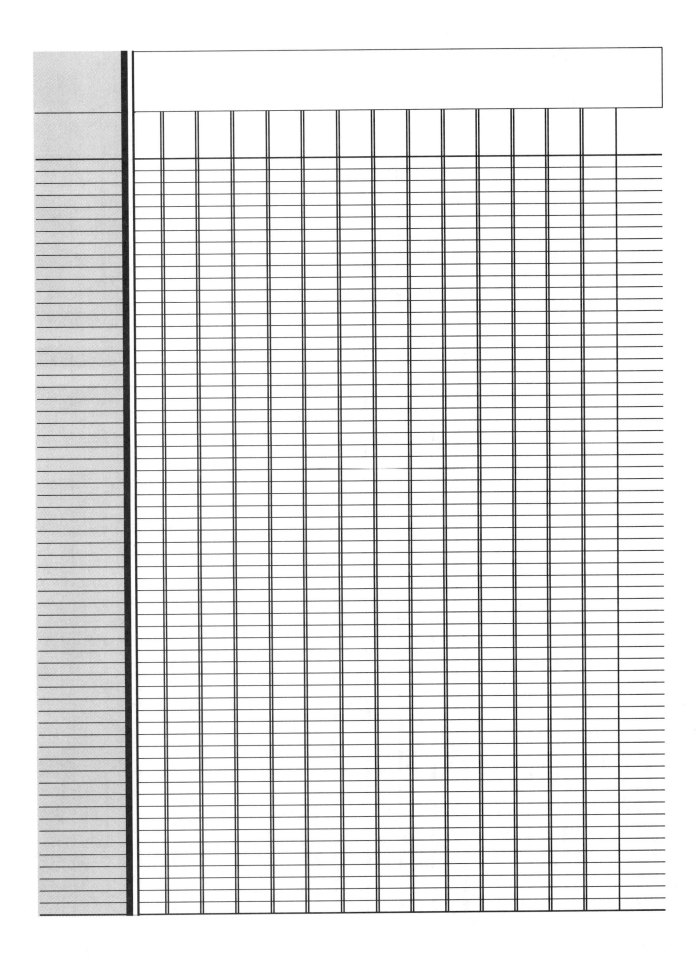

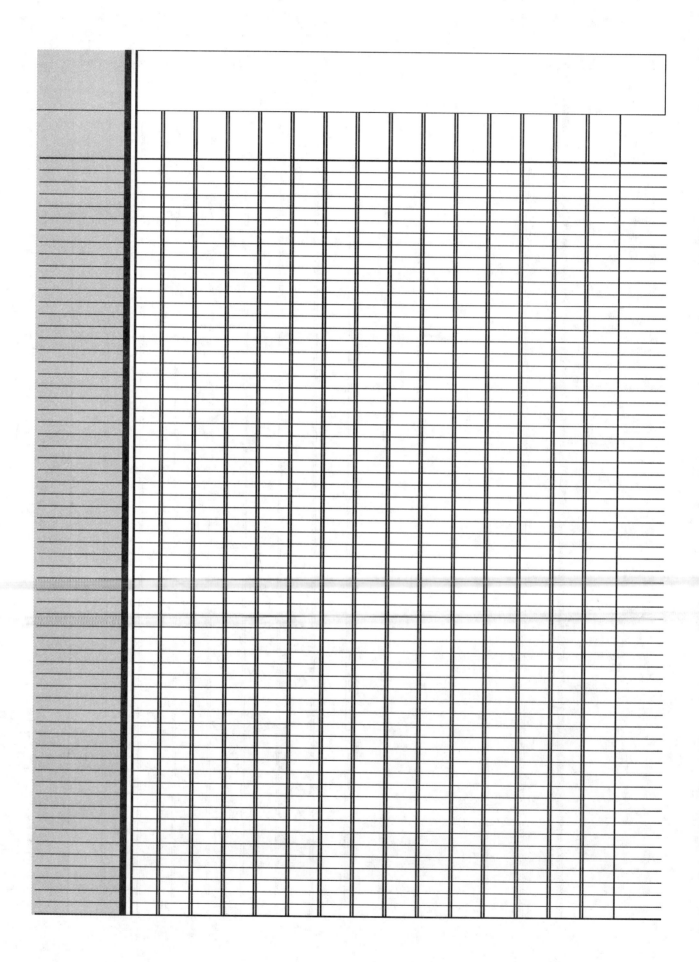

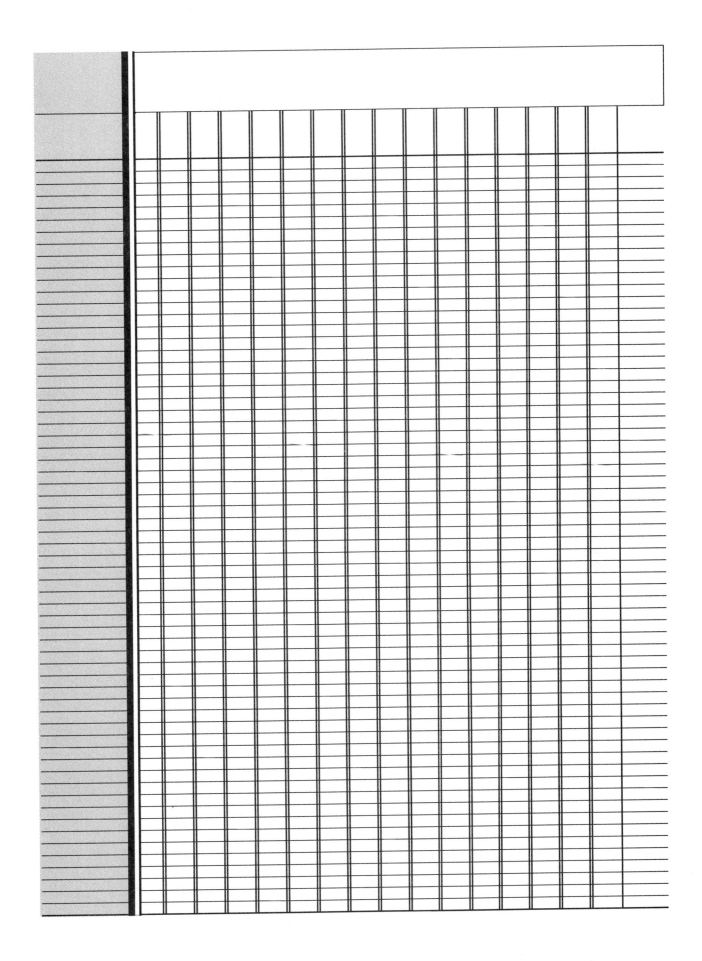

6:00	
6:30	
7:00	
7:30	
8:00	
8:30	
9:00	
9:30	
10:00	
10:30	
11:00	
11:30	
12:00	
12:30	
1:00	
1:30	
2:00	
2:30	
3:00	
3:30	
4:00	
4:30	
5:00	
5:30	

6:00		
6:30		
7:00		
7:30		
8:00		
8:30		
9:00		
9:30		
10:00		
10:30		
11:00		
11:30		
12:00		
12:30		
1:00		
1:30		
2:00		
2:30		
3:00		
3:30		
4:00		
4:30		
5:00		
5:30		

6:00			
6:30			
7:00			
7:30			
8:00			
8:30			
9:00			
9:30			
10:00			
10:30			
11:00			
11:30			
12:00			
12:30			
1:00			
1:30			
2:00			
2:30			
3:00			
3:30			
4:00			
4:30			
5:00			
5:30			

6:00				
6:30				
7:00				
7:30				
8:00				
8:30				
9:00				
9:30				
10:00				
10:30				
11:00				
11:30				
12:00				
12:30				
1:00				
1:30				
2:00				
2:30				
3:00				
3:30				
4:00				
4:30				
5:00				
5:30				

6:00					
6:30					
7:00					
7:30					
8:00					
8:30					
9:00					
9:30					
10:00					
10:30					
11:00					
11:30					
12:00					
12:30					
1:00					
1:30					
2:00					
2:30					
3:00					
3:30					
4:00					
4:30					
5:00					
5:30					

6:00					
6:30					
7:00					
7:30					
8:00					
8:30					
9:00					
9:30					
10:00					
10:30					
11:00					
11:30					
12:00					
12:30					
1:00					
1:30					
2:00					
2:30					
3:00					
3:30					
4:00					
4:30					
5:00					
5:30					

6:00						
6:30						
7:00						
7:30						
8:00						
8:30						
9:00						
9:30						
10:00						
10:30						
11:00						
11:30						
12:00						
12:30						
1:00						
1:30						
2:00						
2:30						
3:00						
3:30						
4:00						
4:30						
5:00						
5:30						

6:00							
6:30							
7:00							
7:30							
8:00							
8:30							
9:00							
9:30							
10:00							
10:30							
11:00							
11:30							
12:00							
12:30							
1:00							
1:30							
2:00							
2:30							
3:00							
3:30							
4:00							
4:30							
5:00							
5:30							

6:00									
6:30									
7:00									
7:30									
8:00									
8:30									
9:00									
9:30									
10:00									
10:30									
11:00									
11:30									
12:00									
12:30									
1:00									
1:30									
2:00									
2:30									
3:00									
3:30									
4:00									
4:30									
5:00									
5:30									

	6:00									
	6:30									
	7:00									
	7:30									
	8:00									
	8:30									
	9:00									
	9:30									
	10:00									
	10:30									
	11:00									
	11:30									
	12:00									
	12:30									
	1:00									
	1:30									
	2:00									
	2:30									
	3:00									
	3:30									
	4:00									
	4:30									
	5:00									
	5:30									

6:00										
6:30										
7:00										
7:30										
8:00										
8:30										
9:00										
9:30										
10:00										
10:30										
11:00										
11:30										
12:00										
12:30										
1:00										
1:30										
2:00										
2:30										
3:00										
3:30										
4:00										
4:30										
5:00										
5:30										

6:00											
6:30											
7:00											
7:30											
8:00											
8:30											
9:00											
9:30											
10:00											
10:30											
11:00											
11:30											
12:00											
12:30											
1:00											
1:30											
2:00											
2:30											
3:00											
3:30											
4:00											
4:30											
5:00											
5:30											

	Sunday	Monday	Tuesday	Wednesday	Thursday	Friday	Saturday	
8:00								8:00
8:30								8:30
9:00								9:00
9:30								9:30
10:00								10:00
10:30								10:30
11:00								11:00
11:30								11:30
12:00								12:00
12:30								12:30
1:00								1:00
1:30								1:30
2:00								2:00
2:30								2:30
3:00								3:00
3:30								3:30
4:00								4:00
4:30								4:30
5:00								5:00
5:30								5:30

	A.M.	P.M.
Sunday		
Monday		
Tuesday		
Wednesday		
Thursday		
Friday		
Saturday		

	Sunday	Monday	Tuesday	Wednesday	Thursday	Friday	Saturday
6:00							
6:15							
6:30							
6:45							
7:00							
7:15							
7:30							
7:45							
8:00							
8:15							
8:30							
8:45							
9:00							
9:15							
9:30							
9:45							
10:00							
10:15							
10:30							
10:45							
11:00							
11:15							
11:30							
11:45							
12:00							
12:15							
12:30							
12:45							
1:00							
1:15							
1:30							
1:45							
2:00							
2:15							
2:30							
2:45							
3:00							
3:15							
3:30							
3:45							
4:00							
4:15							
4:30							
4:45							
5:00							
5:15							
5:30							
5:45							
6:00							

	A.M.	P.M.
Sunday		
Monday		
Tuesday		
Wednesday		
Thursday		
Friday		
Saturday		

	A.M.	P.M.
Sunday		
Monday		
Tuesday		
Wednesday		
Thursday		
Friday		
Saturday		

Monday	
Tuesday	
Wednesday	
Thursday	
Friday	
Monday	
Tuesday	
Wednesday	
Thursday	
Friday	
Monday	
Tuesday	
Wednesday	
Thursday	
Friday	
Monday	
Tuesday	
Wednesday	
Thursday	
Friday	
Monday	
Tuesday	
Wednesday	
Thursday	
Friday	

Monday						
Tuesday						
Wednesday						
Thursday						
Friday						
Monday						
Tuesday						
Wednesday						
Thursday						
Friday						
Monday						
Tuesday						
Wednesday						
Thursday						
Friday						
Monday						
Tuesday						
Wednesday						
Thursday						
Friday						
Monday						
Tuesday						
Wednesday						
Thursday						
Friday						

Monday													
Tuesday													
Wednesday													
Thursday													
Friday													
Monday													
Tuesday													
Wednesday													
Thursday													
Friday													
Monday													
Tuesday													
Wednesday													
Thursday													
Friday													
Monday													
Tuesday													
Wednesday													
Thursday													
Friday													
Monday													
Tuesday													
Wednesday													
Thursday													
Friday													

Week	
1	
2	
3	
4	
5	
6	
7	
8	
9	
10	
11	
12	
13	

Week						
1						
2						
3						
4						
5						
6						
7						
8						
9						
10						
11						
12						
13						

Week												
1												
2												
3												
4												
5												
6												
7												
8												
9												
10												
11												
12												
13												

1
2
3
4
5
6
7
8
9
10
11
12
13
14
15
16
17
18
19
20
21
22
23
24
25
26
27
28
29
30
31
32
33
34
35
36
37
38
39
40
41
42
43
44
45
46
47
48
49
50
51
52

27	28	29	30	31	32	33	34	35	36	37	38	39		40	41	42	43	44	45	46	47	48	49	50	51	52
1	2	3	4	5	6	7	8	9	10	11	12	13		14	15	16	17	18	19	20	21	22	23	24	25	26

Jan.		Jan.
Feb.		Feb.
Mar.		Mar.
Apr.		Apr.
May		May
Jun.		Jun.
Jul.		Jul.
Aug.		Aug.
Sept.		Sept.
Oct.		Oct.
Nov.		Nov.
Dec.		Dec.

Jan.						Jan.
Feb.						Feb.
Mar.						Mar.
Apr.						Apr.
May						May
Jun.						Jun.
Jul.						Jul.
Aug.						Aug.
Sept.						Sept.
Oct.						Oct.
Nov.						Nov.
Dec.						Dec.

	January	February	March	April	May	June	July	August	September	October	November	December		

	January	February	March	April	May	June	July	August	September	October	November	December		

		January	February	March	April	May	June	July	August	September	October	November	December		

	January	February	March	April	May	June	July	August	September	October	November	December	

January	February	March

April	May	June

July	August	September

October	November	December

	January	February	March	April	May	June	July	August	September	October	November	December	

	January	February	March	April	May	June	July	August	September	October	November	December	

27

28

29

30

31

32

33

34

35

36

37

38

39

40

41

42

43

44

45

46

47

48

49

50

51

52

1
2
3
4
5
6
7
8
9
10
11
12
13
14
15
16
17
18
19
20
21
22
23
24
25
26
27
28
29
30
31
32
33
34
35
36
37
38
39
40
41
42
43
44
45
46
47
48
49
50

51
52
53
54
55
56
57
58
59
60
61
62
63
64
65
66
67
68
69
70
71
72
73
74
75
76
77
78
79
80
81
82
83
84
85
86
87
88
89
90
91
92
93
94
95
96
97
98
99
100

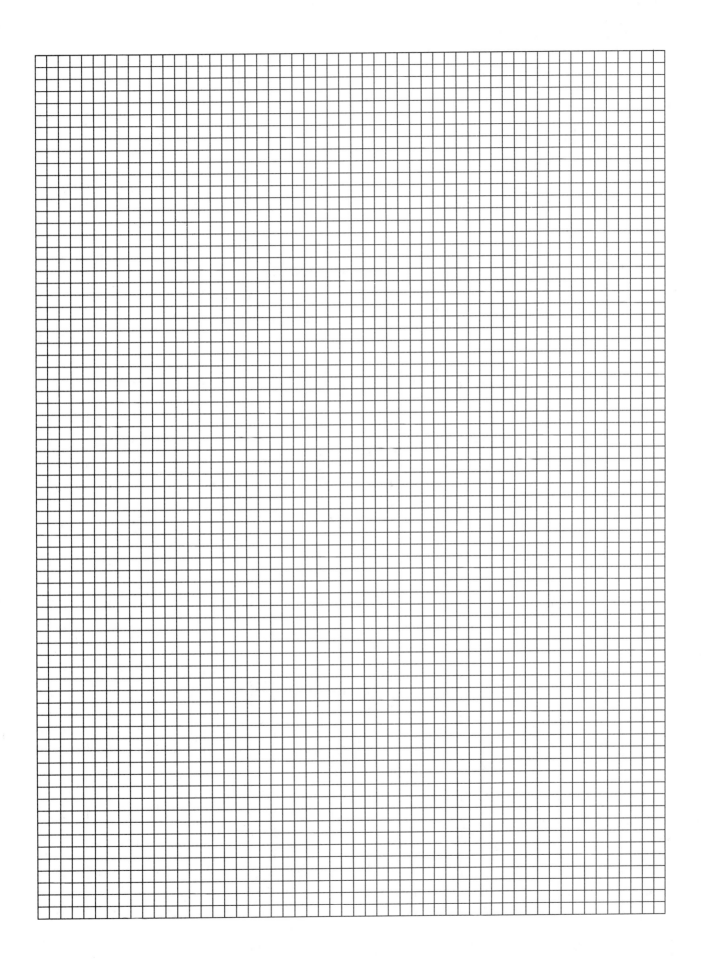

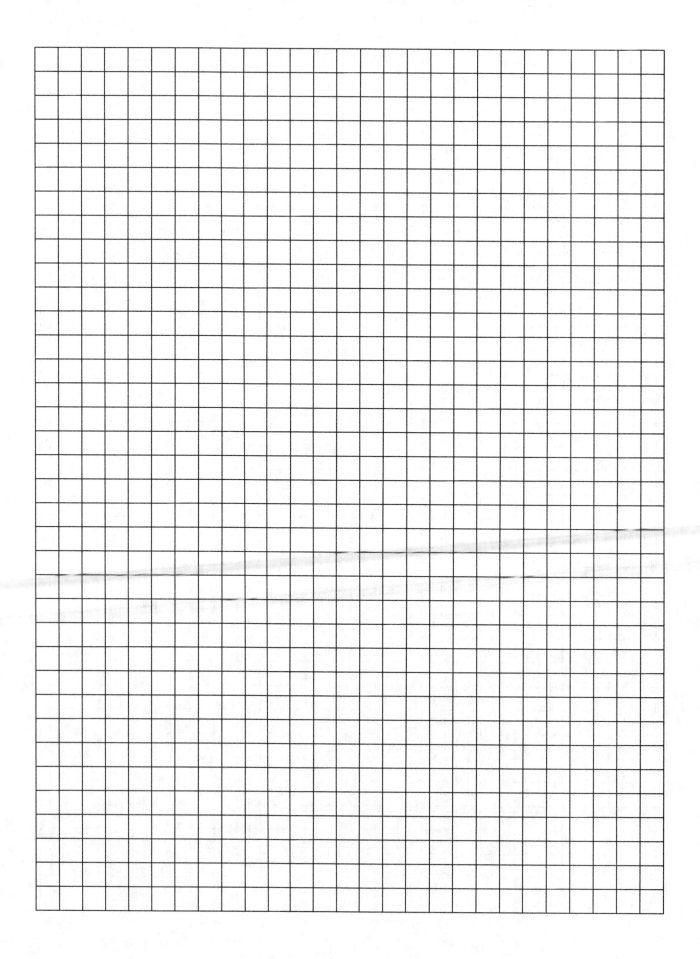